SUB CULTURE

SUB CULTURE
The Many Lives of the Submarine

John Medhurst

REAKTION BOOKS

Published by Reaktion Books Ltd
Unit 32, Waterside
44–48 Wharf Road
London N1 7UX, UK
www.reaktionbooks.co.uk

First published 2022
Copyright © John Medhurst 2022

Printed and bound in Great Britain by TJ Books Ltd, Padstow, Cornwall

A catalogue record for this book is available from the British Library

ISBN 978 1 78914 637 0

CONTENTS

'The Holland boats (early submarines) are interesting novelties which appeal to the non-professional mind, which is apt to invest them with remarkable properties they do not possess. In my opinion, they are ingenious contrived craft of an eccentric character which mark a step in the development of an interesting science but nothing more.'
Rear Admiral Charles O'Neil,
Chief of the u.s. Navy Bureau of Ordnance, 1900

They bear, in place of classic names,
   Letters and numbers on their skin
They play their grisly blindfold games
   In little boxes made of tin.
Rudyard Kipling, 'The Trade', 1916

INTRODUCTION:
THE IMAGE OF A SUBMARINE

The vision of a manned submersible exploring the ocean deeps is an old one. In 332 BCE Alexander the Great is reported to have descended into the Aegean Sea in a glass sphere to observe aquatic life. In the early sixteenth century Leonardo da Vinci sketched plans for a theoretical submarine, as he had for a functioning helicopter. The first realizable submarine schematic, devised by William Bourne in 1578, inspired the Dutch designer Cornelis Drebbel, who in the early seventeenth century secured the interest and funding of King James I to construct a prototype. In 1623 Drebbel's submersible, using leather goatskin bags to vent water, made its erratic passage along the River Thames from Westminster to Greenwich.

None of these inventions found a reflection in the culture of their day. They were bold ideas ahead of their time, radical new technology that had not yet solved the essential dilemma of submersible craft: how to adjust ballast in order to control depth and speed. The first submarines to fully achieve this were built a few hundred years later, in the nineteenth century. They were brutally pragmatic, created not for scientific exploration but to deter and attack the maritime resources of current and future enemies. Yet the original, more idealistic conception of the submarine has endured and has been translated into a rich variety of imaginative fiction.

Rowboat submersible invented by Cornelis Drebbel, illustration by H. A. Naber in *De ster van 1572* (1907).

Sometimes that imaginary conception directly impacts reality. In 1955, one year after the USA had launched the world's first nuclear-powered submarine (the *Nautilus*, named after the first and greatest fictional submarine), its junior ally the UK was desperate to follow suit. For this to happen the head of the British Navy, Lord Mountbatten, needed a budget commitment from the Chancellor of the Exchequer, Derick Heathcoat-Amory. Aware that the chancellor came from an old naval family, Mountbatten constructed a highly detailed 20-inch (51 cm) model of a nuclear submarine, which opened up to display its inner workings, and at the start of the crucial meeting of the Cabinet Defence Committee he placed it on the table in front of him. Heathcoat-Amory was so entranced with the model that he played with it throughout the meeting, only glancing up to ask 'How much?' when asked to approve the required funding. Upon being told the cost, he instantly signed it off.[1]

A number of men (for it is usually men) develop a fascination with the submarine as a singular weapon of war, a high-tech Sword of Damocles hanging over humanity. Yet the first meaningful appearance of the submarine in world culture, in Jules Verne's *Twenty Thousand Leagues Under the Sea* (1870), was not as a weapon of mass destruction but a wonder of imaginative fantasy, a means of expanding humanity's knowledge and experience of its own world. I would argue that this initial, fantastical and utopian concept has rooted itself in public consciousness just as deeply as its subsequent military application.

In 2014 the British novelist Margaret Drabble recalled a childhood Christmas present of an illustrated edition of Verne's classic adventure, and the lifelong effect it had upon her. 'The sense of excitement communicated by Verne more than half a century ago is with me still.'[2] Verne's submarine not only went on to lend its name to the first real-world iterations of its vision, and a host of other innovative oceanographic and maritime exploratory projects, but to embed the template for the steampunk submarine into literary-cultural fashion over a century later.

The romantic image of the submarine, epitomized by the iconic name *Nautilus*, continues to inspire scientific exploration even beyond our planet. In January 2019 the Nautilus Deep Space Observatory

(NDSO), a proposed fleet of space telescopes using extremely lightweight telescope mirrors for enhanced data capture, designed to search for the bio-signatures of alien life in the atmosphere of planets that orbit other stars, received initial funding to construct a prototype. If successful, the NDSO could eventually replace the Hubble Space Telescope as Earth's gateway to the cosmos.

The Earth-bound submarine is still capable of generating excitement but not necessarily the excitement of wonder and discovery. Its more common image in contemporary culture is that of a highly sophisticated weapon of mass destruction, suitably packaged and glamorized to support militaristic political agendas. The popular submarine-themed blog The Lean Submariner, run by a retired U.S. Navy Chief Warrant Officer who served on five nuclear-powered submarines during his career, runs the gamut of submarine fandom, from the history of American nuclear submarines to useful advice about post-traumatic stress disorder.

With over half a million visits since its inception, The Lean Submariner showcases a host of 'submarine memes for the new millennium' for the enjoyment of veterans and armchair warriors alike. These include a range of self-congratulatory and politically questionable slogans such as 'Today, not a single submariner took a knee to draw attention to themselves. They were too busy protecting the lives of those who do', or, superimposed over photographs of nuclear submarines at sea, 'When I was nineteen, this was my "safe space". No-one gave it to us. We made it that way. 'The politics are resolutely Republican – 'The politicians keep telling us we can't possibly kill all the terrorists and diplomacy will eventually work. I'm willing to take the chance that using enough of these just *might* kill the ones who are coming for my family.' These memes ricochet around the Internet and social media in the company of similar alt-right material attacking liberals, feminists and 'woke' culture.[3]

Alan Moore, author of *Watchmen* and *The League of Extraordinary Gentlemen* and a considerable cultural anthropologist in his own right, believes that ideas, images and archetypes exist in a meaningful and literal sense, and formulated the concept of 'idea space' to encompass them. The submarine, as an abstract concept, has a place there. Moore's friend and sometime collaborator in psychogeography Iain Sinclair, in his book on the metaphysical significance of a day's walk around the circumference of London's Overground rail network, tells of a train passing by late in the evening, towards the end of a 56-kilometre (35 mi.) trek: 'A late Overground train, windows illuminated by an uncanny storm-light glow, ferried a party of circling warlocks across the Camden Road bridge: a Jules Verne submarine out of its element.'[4]

Sinclair often taps into idea space. In creating the original *Nautilus*, Verne not only drew from it but added to its substratum. Even Mountbatten dabbled with it when he gave Heathcoat-Amory an ideal of a submarine to play with in order to secure billions of pounds to translate it into reality. In their own way, so do The Lean Submariner and similar blogs and websites that trade in the mythology and imagery of the modern nuclear submarine.

Military history, film theory and media and communication studies have all in different ways and with different emphasis considered the importance and influence of the submarine. But no one work has fused these analytical techniques together for a panoptic view. The nearest equivalent to this approach, dealing with a not-unrelated subject, is Patrick Wright's monumental cultural history *Tank* (2001), which traces the social impact and semiotics of the tank from the First World War to Tiananmen Square.

Wright argues that the tank is more than just a piece of military hardware. While *Tank* fully explains its immense military import, from the Somme to the Battle of Kursk (an epic six-week battle in 1943 between Nazi Germany and the Soviet Union, involving thousands of tanks on either side, which military historians consider the hinge-point of the Second World War) to its crucial role in the Arab–Israeli Six-Day War, he extends its analysis into art, mythology, psychology and culture. He presents the tank in the round and reveals a machine that has morphed from an exhilarating experiment in techno-futurism to the ultimate symbol of brutal state repression.

Wright's book set a high standard and justified its tank-like bulk. By contrast *Sub Culture* approaches its subject like its subject – sleeker, quicker, under the radar. It explores the story of the submarine from the American Civil War to the 2020s, stressing its central and determinative role in the two World Wars and the Cold War. It situates it at the centre of modern history and international politics, the geostrategic equivalent of antibiotics in health care and the smartphone in communications. It also seeks to illuminate the submarine's history through its representation in pulp and mainstream literature and in popular and esoteric art and film, from Rudyard Kipling to *The Hunt for Red October*.

Cultural theory does not ignore the intrinsic qualities of individual works but its primary purpose is to deconstruct them to suggest how cultural production – whether film, novel, poem, popular music, comic or cartoon – is related to the systems of political and ideological power within which they arise. With the submarine this is not difficult. The submarine is not one of the great generic themes of human art. It is an enormous, expensive machine that can only be constructed by those with power and wealth. It achieves significance through the political uses to which it is put and through its role in scientific and technological discovery.

Nevertheless an identifiable narrative genre, a specific cultural mythos, has emerged from popular experience and perception of the submarine. It fuses elements of mainstream genres such as military adventure, historical drama, political thriller and espionage to form a unique hybrid, although its individual products vary greatly in style and content.

It is arguable that this genre appeals to primarily Western audiences. It is these wealthier, technologically advanced countries that have built submarine fleets and deployed them widely, thereby absorbing them into their society's fiction and imagination. These representations will have less resonance and meaning for societies that have not them- selves produced submarines, or for whom they are mainly a status symbol for a political-military elite divorced from their nation's social reality. A contemporary submarine film such as *Hunter Killer* (2018), set on a modern American nuclear sub, assumes a certain kind of audience receptivity. To the poor of the Global South it may as well be about a mission to Jupiter.

Although today the BRIC nations – Brazil, Russia, India and China, plus others such as Iran and North Korea – possess substantial submarine fleets, for most of the twentieth century it was the 'core' Western nations that led the way. The glaring exception to this was Soviet Russia, whose fleet of nuclear-powered submarines engaged in Cold War shadow-boxing with its U.S. and NATO equivalents for four decades, occasionally skirting close to total war.

The financial and technological resources required to build and maintain submarine fleets mean they are invariably arms of the state, specifically the naval forces of nations that possess the financial resources required to construct or purchase them. While these navies contain a range of submersibles engaged in useful scientific research work, that work is usually conducted under the aegis of the state and its superstructural academic institutions.

That the modern submarine is primarily a tool of the military limits the issues a drama set within it can explore. While it is certainly possible to imagine a fictional narrative that questions the entire utility and purpose of a nuclear submarine fleet, such a narrative would mostly take place in the wider civilian world. On-board stories could not fully explore the complexities and compromises of a civilian democratic polity. As the American nuclear submarine captain says in the 1995 film *Crimson Tide*, 'We preserve democracy, not practice it.'

This political fault line cannot be ignored. The comfortable fit of the modern submarine techno-thriller with the ideological values of Fox News must give all enthusiasts for the genre pause. But that ethos was not always dominant. The best-selling naval and submarine adventures of Douglas Reeman and Alexander Fullerton, the best of which were written between the 1950s and the 1980s, were neither as politically reactionary nor as drenched in machismo. Today, the most radical challenge to the constraints of the genre comes not from the military thriller but from science fiction and fantasy novels, comics and films, where the submarine is not as encumbered by superpower politics and is sometimes overtly critical of them.

Despite the high standards set by Reeman and Fullerton, and excellent submarine-themed paintings from artists such as Philip Connard, Roderick Macdonald and Stephen Bone, the subject's most visible expression – big-budget films produced by the American and British film industries in the twentieth and twenty-first centuries – are clearly not driven by pure artistic impulse. From the 1920s to the end of the Cold War, the USA and UK almost entirely dominated these products. Inevitably, they reflect a hegemonic ideology. Even the most famous counter-example, *Das Boot*, was a reaction against that dominance, a powerful eulogy for the losers of a global imperialist struggle but not a challenge to the system that created it.

Hence the marginal nature of entries in the submarine genre from the junior and defeated participants in the fight for global dominance, such as Japan and Russia. Russia's forays into the genre have been belated and defensive, echoing its rush to catch up in the real world, the lower quality of the Soviet Union's technology compared to that of the USA, and the subsequent accidents and disasters that have dogged their submarine fleet (evidenced in the tragic accidents portrayed in films like *K19: The Widowmaker, Hostile Waters, Kursk* and Russia's own *72 Meters*).

Other countries have explored the genre in a manner that reflects the position of the submarine within their history and culture. Japan, although it fielded a large submarine fleet in the Pacific during the Second World War, including the largest submarine ever built until the construction of ballistic missile submarines in the 1960s, is not attracted to the 'realistic' submarine drama of the Western film industry. Rather, it has mutated the submarine into a variety of post-apocalyptic, semi-sentient machines in numerous manga and anime products. India, by contrast, despite having a film industry to rival Hollywood, has virtually ignored the genre. Its first submarine movie, *The Ghazi Attack*, was produced in 2017.

Social class runs through the submarine genre as it runs through the vessel itself, from the captain's cabin and the officer's wardroom to the engine room. Like all parts of the armed services, the submarine operates with a clear hierarchy. The failure of that hierarchy to fully function is often at the core of the conventional submarine drama, as exemplified in two of its most outstanding products, the American films *Crimson Tide* and *Run Silent, Run Deep*.

And yet, while the necessity of rigid job specification is essential if the submarine is to operate safely, a submarine carries no senior officers. During both world wars a submarine's 'captain' was often a lieutenant given the title of captain for the duration of the mission only. Relatively speaking, it is the more proletarian part of the military services. The conditions on board a submarine tend to a rough equality. A submarine, once at sea, is a great leveller.

The same cannot be said of gender. Until the BBC's game-changing TV drama *Vigil* (2021), the accepted parameters of the submarine genre had excluded women from anything other than supporting roles, although there was no reason why narratives based around scientific exploration or the wider social lives of a submarine's crew could not include strong, leading female characters. In the meantime, while submarine dramas seldom address sexual or gender issues directly, they contain a wealth of incidental references to women and sex that are all the more revealing because of their indirect and casual nature. And in a wider sense the choice of this specific genre – that is, of a narrative vehicle without significant female characters – by an author or film studio to sell a novel or attract a mass audience is itself a matter of gender politics.

Sub Culture's analysis of the submarine is developed in six thematic chapters that overlap and cross-refer. These chapters consider the submarine as a weapon of war, a political instrument, a doomsday device, a vehicle for scientific exploration, a product of fantasy and imagination, and a context for sexism and homophobia. The format is designed to construct a holistic portrait of the submarine in which geo-strategic politics, technology, science and culture interact. A conclusion draws these elements together and predicts how the submarine and the fictional genre that has grown up around it may develop and transform during the twenty-first century.

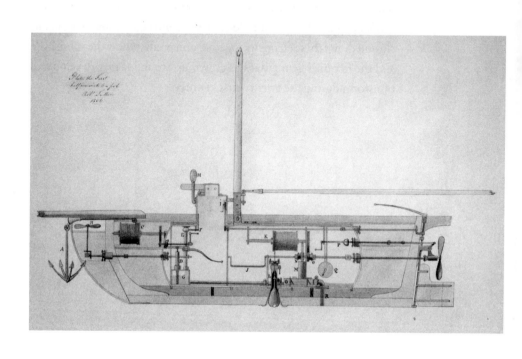

1

THE SUBMARINE IN WAR

The submarine as commonly understood – that is, not a simple bathysphere lowered into the ocean and pulled back up again but a self-propelling undersea vehicle – was mainly a theoretical exercise until the use of David Bushnell's *Turtle* submersible by American Revolutionary forces in 1776. The *Turtle*, the first 'submarine' to be deployed in combat, used water as ballast and a screw propeller at its rear, both methods still in use today. Although it failed in its attempted missions to attach explosives to the underside of British warships, the *Turtle* put down a marker for the future of warfare.

That future arrived in the form of the 'plunging boat' *Nautilus*, widely considered the first practical submarine ever constructed. Designed between 1793 and 1797 for the French First Republic, it was the brainchild of the American engineer Robert Fulton, inventor of the first commercially successful steamboat. Built of copper sheets attached to iron ribs, on which sat two horizontal diving pins to control the angle of descent, the *Nautilus* was propelled by a hand-cranked screw propeller. In trials at Le Havre harbour in 1801 Fulton took the *Nautilus* down 7.6 metres (25 ft) and stayed submerged for an hour.

Like the *Turtle*, the *Nautilus* was supposed to attach mines to enemy ships, but it never had the opportunity to achieve its potential. Unfortunately, like all inventors ahead of their time, Fulton lacked the technical resources to realize his plans. When Napoleon tired of him he took his invention to Britain, where it was equally unappreciated,

Design schematic of Robert Fulton's *Nautilus*, 1806.

although on Prime Minister Pitt the Younger's instructions he did produce a new range of sea-based assault weapons, including the first modern torpedoes.

In 1861 the French inventor Brutus de Villeroi, Fulton's successor in pushing submarine design as far as the technology of his day would allow, tried to persuade President Lincoln that the submarine would provide the North with a weapon to win the Civil War. Lincoln was not impressed but de Villeroi, when a professor of mathematics at Nantes University in the early 1840s, had already made a convert arguably more important than Lincoln: his young student Jules Verne, who absorbed his lessons and channelled them into his vision of Captain Nemo's *Nautilus* in *Twenty Thousand Leagues Under the Sea* (1870).

The first successful use of a submarine in warfare was made by a historically reactionary state fighting a losing battle – the Confederate States of America (CSA) in 1864. The American Civil War began in April 1861 when the Confederacy bombarded Fort Sumter, which stood guard over the South Carolina port of Charleston. Thereafter Charleston was integral to the struggle between North and South. Needing a means to break the U.S. Navy's blockade, which was strangling the South's trade in cotton and its ability to fund its rebellion, the Confederacy turned, in some desperation, to submarines.

In March 1862 a New Orleans consortium headed by Horace L. Hunley was granted permission to build a submarine capable of sinking blockade ships. Their first effort was named the *Pioneer*. The design of the *Pioneer* was crude, essentially a 20-foot-long (6 m) iron tube propelled by hand cranks and manually adjusted diving planes that could tow a mine under an enemy ship. Early trials attacking barges showed promise but the lack of ventilation meant that even a small crew could not stay submerged for longer than five minutes without having to come up for air. Efforts to solve this were cut short in April 1862 when Northern forces took New Orleans and the *Pioneer* was scuttled in Lake Pontchartrain to prevent it falling into their hands.

The next attempt was the CSS *Hunley*, named after its backer. Constructed from an old steam boiler, the *Hunley* was 40 feet (12 m) long with stern and aft ballast tanks, a hand-cranked propeller and a small periscope. In its initial trials the boat sank twice, the second time drowning all aboard, including Hunley. However, with Charleston suffering heavy bombardment and near to collapse, the Southern commander General P.G.T. Beauregard ordered a third attempt be made under the command of Lieutenant George Dixon.

This was more successful. On 17 February 1864 the *Hunley* submerged in Charleston harbour and made its way at periscope depth to the blockade ship USS *Housatonic*, ramming a remote-triggered spar torpedo into its hull. It backed off before detonation, but still the resulting explosion sank the *Hunley* as well as the *Housatonic*. Although all the *Hunley*'s crew were killed, they had made military history as the first submarine to sink an enemy ship in wartime.

Conrad Wise
Chapman,
*Submarine Torpedo
Boat H. L. Hunley,
6 December 1863,*
1864, oil on panel.

The *Hunley* was eventually resurrected, in actuality and in film. In 1995 an expedition funded by the thriller writer Clive Cussler discovered the lost submarine on the seabed near the wreck of the *Housatonic*. Cussler, author of the best-selling adventures of Dirk Pitt and the fictional National Underwater and Marine Agency (NUMA), used the proceeds of his novels to create a real-world NUMA, a non-profit organization to find and salvage underwater wrecks. Four years after a NUMA diving team found and photographed the wreck of the *Hunley*, it was carefully raised and put on display in Charleston.[1]

Thanks to Cussler's operation the story of the *Hunley*, largely forgotten outside the ranks of Civil War enthusiasts, returned to public consciousness and was translated into drama in the American TV film *The Hunley* (1999) starring Armand Assante as Lieutenant Dixon and Donald Sutherland as General Beauregard. The film hits many sound notes, in particular its portrayal of the erosion of civilian morale in a

H. L. Hunley in its water tank at Clemson University in North Charleston, South Carolina, 2012.

Charleston under daily bombardment from Union ships. Assante's weary Dixon is a sympathetic hero, ready to take the *Hunley* out again even though its first two attempts drowned its crews. Yet, for a film made in the post-civil rights era, it retains the disabling flaw of many submarine movies. It lauds the courage of the men inside the boat without examining the dubious political cause for which they died.

The film's central characters, Dixon and Beauregard, regard themselves as 'romantics in an age of barbarians', but it is the film itself that is inexcusably romantic. However significant the *Hunley*'s attack on the *Housatonic* was in the annals of naval warfare, further successes of this type would have lengthened the war and the institution of Southern slavery. The film shows slaves only once, cleaning mud off the *Hunley* after it has been dredged from the bottom of the river. The lives of the *Hunley*'s crew matter in a way that Black lives do not.

The years between the American Civil War and the First World War saw huge advances in submarine technology, due almost entirely to the innovations of the engineer John Philip Holland. In the 1870s Holland, an Irishman who had emigrated to America, took his ideas about submarine design to the U.S. Navy but without success. He turned next to the well-heeled American wing of the Irish Revolutionary Brotherhood (IRB), or the Fenians. Holland's first attempt at a submarine for the IRB, the *Fenian Ram*, was hampered by technical problems but his innovative concepts, including a compressed air system to launch torpedoes and an on-board toilet, took the submarine far beyond the converted steam boiler of the *Hunley* era.

Holland's new designs finally bore fruit when the U.S. Navy, beginning to wake up to the potential of the submarine for coastal defence and covert attack missions, held the first of three separate competitions (1887, 1888 and 1893) for the best and most efficient submarine design. Holland won all three, but funding was held up by sceptics and political infighting. Finally, in 1895 the John P. Holland Torpedo Boat Company was awarded a contract to build a version of Holland's newest design for a 54-foot-long (16.5 m) vessel that could dive safely to 100 feet (30 m).

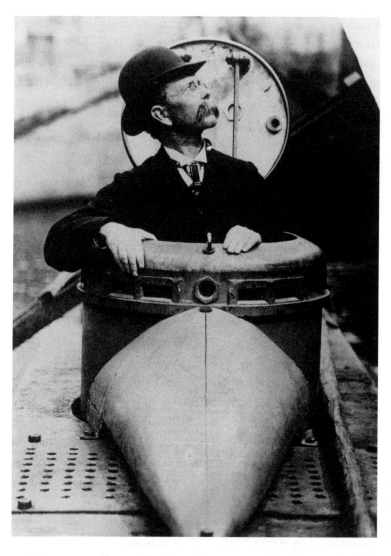

John Philip Holland
in the conning tower
of the submarine
Holland (later uss
Holland), c. 1898–9.

There was still considerable resistance to authorizing money for
more than one submarine, but the Congressional hearings convened to
examine the matter were swayed by the testimony of Captain Alfred T.
Mahan, whose *The Influence of Seapower upon History, 1660–1783*, published in 1892, was widely regarded as the definitive work on grand naval
strategy. Mahan was concerned that the u.s. Navy, which had shrunk

considerably since the Civil War, was tiny in comparison to those of rivals such as Britain, Germany and France, and needed something to redress the balance. Holland's money was voted through after Mahan observed, 'In our present unprotected position, the risk of losing the money by virtue of the boat's being a failure is more than counterbalanced by the great protection the boat would be if a substantial success.'

Launch of HMS *Holland* 1 at Barrow-in-Furness, UK, October 1901.

First *Holland* boat used by the U.S. Navy, c. 1900.

Mahan had the insight to see that Holland had developed a fully functioning submarine that ticked all the boxes for its successful use: a firm outer hull and an even firmer inner hull to protect the crew from the immense water pressure the lower it dived; reliable ballast and trim tanks to control buoyancy and keep its weight perfectly balanced; rudder controls and diving planes to control its rise and descent. To these Holland added an internal combustion engine for running on the surface and charging batteries, and a crude Electro-Dynamic electric motor for submerged operations. His prototype, *Holland VI*, could attain a speed of 6 knots when surfaced and 5.5 knots when submerged.

Launched in 1897, *Holland VI* was the basis for submarine design through the first half of the twentieth century. Even so, it still used an unreliable petrol engine, could not stay submerged for very long without running out of oxygen and was notorious for containing a toilet that often overflowed back into the boat. These things would improve over time. It entered service with the u.s. Navy in 1900 as uss *Holland*, and was subsequently given the number ss1, the u.s. Navy's first submarine.[2]

The British Royal Navy, aware that America and France were investing in this new technology, promptly hired Holland's company, now renamed the Electric Boat Company, to build five submarines. As a result the Royal Navy's first submarine, the 63-foot-long (19 m) HMS *Holland 1*, was launched in October 1901.[3] By 1910 Britain had 61 Holland-type submarines. In 1904 France pulled ahead with the *Aigrette*, the first submarine to use a diesel engine on the surface and an electric engine below. Diesel engines burned oil instead of gas and so produced fewer toxic fumes but were useless underwater because they needed air for combustion, hence the need for electric battery propulsion as well. The *Aigrette*'s design was immediately copied by the u.s. Navy's new Skipjack-class submarines, one of which, the *E-1*, became the first American submarine to cross the Atlantic under her own power.

Germany, which under its new emperor, Wilhelm II, was desperate to create an overseas empire to rival the UK's, did not fail to notice what its rivals were doing. In 1906 Grand Admiral Tirpitz commissioned the first *Unterseeboot* (Undersea-boat), or U-boat. By 1914 Germany possessed 29 U-boats as against Britain's 77, but unlike Britain's submarines, Germany's were nearly all powered by diesel engines. This meant they could travel more than 5,000 nautical miles (9,260 km) from base and dive deeper than other submarines. They were the first genuine stealth technology, a threat that Britain's naval strategists completely failed to foresee. Even the forward-thinking First Sea Lord, Admiral Sir John Fisher, saw submarines as mainly coastal defence weapons.

Sir Arthur Conan Doyle's short story 'Danger!', published in July 1914 but written in 1912, had a sharper vision. 'Danger!' correctly predicted Germany's U-boat strategy in a future war by suggesting that the fictional country of Norland (that is, Germany) would be able to defeat the UK even after British armies had invaded its territory by using its submarine fleet to blockade British ports. At the climax of the story a Norland submarine torpedoes an American civilian ship bringing essential supplies into Liverpool. With its food supply cut off, Britain has no option but to surrender.

Conan Doyle was soon vindicated. On 15 September 1914, less than two months after the outbreak of war, U-boat *U-21*, submerged off the Firth of Forth, torpedoed the British cruiser *Pathfinder*, hitting its main magazine and igniting a massive explosion. Of the 268 crew, only twelve survived. On 22 September worse followed when the *U-9* torpedoed three British cruisers in rapid succession. Sixteen hundred British sailors died in this one engagement, more than were lost by Admiral Nelson in all of his battles combined.

The British were further humiliated on 23 November when a lone U-boat, *U-18*, appeared in the middle of Scapa Flow in the Orkneys, the main fleet anchorage of the Grand Fleet. Luckily for the British the fleet was at sea and *U-18* was rammed by two coastal defence ships, but the fact that a U-boat with the capacity to destroy its prize Dreadnoughts could so easily penetrate its inner sanctum was a profound blow to Royal Navy morale.[4]

SUBMARINE "U-14"

There was little in the way of defence against submarine attack. In 1914 what would come to be known as anti-submarine warfare (ASW) had not yet been formulated. Sonar was more than a decade away. Hydrophones to detect submarine propeller noise were not deployed until 1916, depth charges (high explosives sealed in barrels and set to detonate at different depths) until 1917. Without these resources the British could deploy only mines and nets, and extra gunnery on battleships to deter U-boats on the surface.

These crude ASW tactics were simply not enough against U-boats seeking to disrupt merchant shipping destined for the UK in the Atlantic

German U-Boat U-14, c. 1912.

and the Mediterranean. Even before its land-based campaign ground to a halt in the trenches of the Western Front, the long-term prospect for the war looked increasingly bleak for the British. Only the use of Q-ships (named after their home port of Queenstown, Ireland) offered a means of taking the fight to the U-boats. A Q-ship was disguised to resemble an easy target such as a lone tramp steamer traversing a region where U-boats were known to operate. They were designed to trick a U-boat into surfacing to attack its target with its deck guns, thus conserving its limited store of torpedoes. Once the U-boat had surfaced, hidden panels on the hull of the Q-ship would drop to reveal its own formidable deck guns, which would then open fire on the exposed submarine.

Despite its neutrality, America found itself embroiled in the escalating U-boat campaign. In April 1915, following Germany's declaration of unrestricted submarine warfare (USW) against *any* ships that might be thought to contain supplies for the UK, the German Embassy in Washington, DC, placed fifty notices in American newspapers warning that all civilians travelling in an 'exclusion zone' around Great Britain and Ireland did so at their own risk.

On 7 May 1915 U-boat *U-20* torpedoed the passenger liner RMS *Lusitania* 20 kilometres (11 mi.) off the coast of Ireland, inside Germany's declared exclusion zone. No direct warning to the target had been given. The liner sank quickly, with 1,198 of the 1,962 complement drowned. One hundred and twenty-four of the dead were American civilians.

Germany justified the sinking by pointing out that the *Lusitania* was officially registered as an armed merchant cruiser and was carrying rifle munitions destined for the UK, and therefore was a legitimate target.

The sinking of the *Lusitania* did not propel America into the war. A large anti-war movement, based partly on socialist anti-imperialism and partly on American isolationism, forced the Democratic president, Woodrow Wilson, to imply that if he were re-elected in 1916 he would keep the USA out of the conflict. His election slogan 'He Kept Us Out of War' was instrumental in his victory (few noticed the past tense). However, since the outbreak of war in 1914 Britain had become the major market for American goods and for loans at interest, with J. P. Morgan acting as a financial agent for the Allies with the U.S. government. With Britain in debt to Morgan for $400 million, American finance had a direct vested interest in a British victory.[5]

Henry Reuterdahl, cover illustration of A. Conan Doyle, *Danger! A Remarkable Story of England at War*, published in *Collier's: The National Weekly*, LIII/23 (22 August 1914).

Unfortunately for those elements in American finance pushing for intervention on Britain's side, Wilson's re-election coincided with the release of the immensely successful film *Civilization* (1916), one of the most ambitious examples of silent cinema, costing the then-unprecedented sum of $1 million to make. The film's poster promised that it 'Vividly Pictures the Modern Menace of SUBMARINE WARFARE'.

An epic allegory about war and pacifism, *Civilization* is set in the imaginary country of Wredpryd (like Conan Doyle's Norland, clearly meant to be Germany), which is plunged into war with a close naval rival. The film's central character, the idealistic Count Ferdinand, is the designer and captain of an advanced prototype submarine ordered to sink a civilian liner believed to be carrying munitions to the enemy. But Ferdinand, a devout Christian, scuttles the submarine with all on board, himself included.

This is merely the overture to *Civilization*'s pacifist message. His soul retrieved by Jesus himself, Ferdinand is sent back to deliver a message of Christian peace to humanity. However, the message is rejected and Ferdinand is condemned to death. The king of Wredpryd visits him in prison but finds him already dead, replaced by Christ, who shows the king the battlefields of Flanders in all their carnage. Shocked, the king signs a peace treaty and the soldiers gratefully return home.

The parallels with the European war and the sinking of the *Lusitania* were obvious. *Civilization*'s battlefield scenes were realistic, fluid and kinetic, and it hammered home its message with zealous glee – a typically lurid screen caption tells us, 'Blood spurting from their wounds, they pray for death.' Released in cinemas in June 1916, the film was a massive box-office success and was credited with helping to secure Wilson's re-election.

On 4 February 1917 Germany reopened USW against any and all ships, including civilian and merchant shipping, that might be carrying munitions or other resources to Britain. The final straw for America was the sinking by U-boat on 25 February 1917 of the Cunard liner RMS *Laconia*. Although casualties were light, a report by a *Chicago Tribune* reporter who was on board the vessel of the deaths of an American mother and daughter led to strident demands for the USA to declare war on Germany. Three weeks later it did so and *Civilization* was pulled from all cinemas.

From 1914 to 1917 the UK government feared that food and other essential supplies would be so disrupted by the U-boats that Britain would have to surrender. The German U-boat fleet, already formidable, was enhanced by a number of 'Cruiser Submarines', extremely large submarines with large cannons on their hulls, able to stay at sea for extended periods. Although these were limited in number – Germany had only three of the new Type *U-139* and seven converted merchant submarines – they were each armed with two 15-centimetre (5.9 in.) guns and patrolled areas far distant from their North Sea bases.

In the end Britain survived only because it started to move its merchant ships in heavily protected naval convoys. This cut its losses by 90 per cent (although even then the cruiser submarines wrought havoc on the convoys). That, and the arrival of large American land forces in 1918, led to Allied victory, but the extent to which Britain had narrowly avoided defeat was not acknowledged for many years.[6] Nor did those who died in the submarine struggle receive a public eulogy, as the officers and men of the British Expeditionary Force in France and Belgium had done. No Wilfred Owen or Siegfried Sassoon lamented the waste of brave young men on and beneath the waves.

While Owen, Sassoon and other war poets had little respect for the military per se – only for the men used as pawns by 'scarlet Majors at the Base', who 'speed glum heroes up the line to death'[7] – there was one significant British poet with a deep regard for the entire culture of the armed forces. By 1914 Rudyard Kipling was world famous for works such as *Plain Tales from the Hills*, *Barrack-Room Ballads* and *The Jungle Book*, and in 1907 he had been awarded the Nobel Prize in Literature. Politically a romantic Conservative and a staunch Ulster Unionist, he had spent the last decade warning of the ambitions of imperial Germany.

In 1915 Kipling was asked by the *Daily Telegraph* to write a series of patriotic articles on the less regarded parts of the Royal Navy, including coastal patrol boats and submarines. Titled 'The Fringes of the Fleet', each article was prefaced by a poem on their theme created for the series. The article 'Submarines' was accompanied by Kipling's short poem 'Tin Fish', with its memorable opening stanza:

> The ships destroy us above
> And ensnare us beneath,
> We arise, we lie down, and we move
> In the belly of Death.

J. H. Cassel, 'Just Like That!', drawing of Kaiser Wilhelm tearing up a paper stating 'Germany's promise to United States to abandon ruthless submarine policy', reproduced in *Evening World Daily Magazine*, 2 February 1917.

In 1916 the articles were reproduced in the book *Sea Warfare*, with an entirely new section on submarines titled 'Tales of the Trade', prefaced by a new poem, 'The Trade'. Kipling's major work on submarine warfare, 'The Trade' granted First World War-era submarines a brief level of cultural acknowledgement:

They bear, in place of classic names,
    Letters and numbers on their skin.
They play their grisly blindfold games
    In little boxes made of tin.

Sometimes they stalk the Zeppelin,
Sometimes they learn where mines are laid,
  Or where the Baltic ice is thin.
That is the custom of 'The Trade.'

Kipling even suggested that submarine crews did not receive enough recognition for the vital role they played in the war effort:

Their feats, their fortunes and their fames
  Are hidden from their nearest kin;
No eager public backs or blames
  No journal prints the yarns they spin
  (The Censor would not let it in!)
When they return from run or raid
  Unheard they work, unseen they win
That is the custom of 'The Trade.'

Following the publication of *Sea Warfare*, Admiral Charles Beresford asked Sir Edward Elgar to translate Kipling's verses into song. Elgar, revered by the British establishment for patriotic compositions such as the five marches *Pomp and Circumstance* (one of which is known in the United States as the graduation march), chose four of the poems, including 'Tin Fish', which he renamed 'Submarines'. The songs were performed at the London Coliseum in June 1917 and then all around the country, with great success. Elgar's last great war-themed composition, they were later recorded by symphony orchestra under the title *The Fringes of the Fleet*.

With the exception of Kipling's poems, Elgar's musical translations and a series of commissioned oil paintings of naval subjects by Philip Connard, virtually all the cultural by-products of First World War submarine warfare are retrospective. The majority of films about or involving submarines in the First World War were produced during the 1920s and '30s. The significant exception was *The Little American* (1917), directed by Cecil B. DeMille, which reflected back to the American psyche its own fear and outrage over German USW.

The heroine, Angela (Mary Pickford), who is at the centre of a pre-war love triangle between herself and two men (one French, one German), finds herself aboard a *Lusitania*-type passenger ship sunk by a U-boat on the outbreak of war in 1917. Barely surviving, she lands in war-torn France, where she is nearly raped by lascivious German soldiers. *The Little American* is a war propaganda film with an explicit message – Germany, whether on land or sea, was the enemy of civilized values.

By the 1930s the USA, which had lost only two submarines in the last war, was losing interest in submarines as a dramatic focus. Other American films of submarine warfare made during the interwar years have more perspective but less emotional investment than *The Little American*. *Submarine* (1928) and *Hell Below* (1933) are slight tales in which two submariners vie for the same woman but come together in adversity at sea. Both films eschew politics or grand humanistic statements for simplistic melodrama. When the last submarine film of the interwar years, *The Spy in Black* (1939), was released, the next war was already inevitable.

The Spy in Black deserves reappraisal not only as the first collaboration of Michael Powell and Emeric Pressburger before their later masterpieces *The Life and Death of Colonel Blimp* (1943), *A Matter of Life and Death* (1946) and *Black Narcissus* (1947), but as a British film made on the eve of the Second World War looking back at the First, which makes no concession at all to nationalistic feeling. Everything is seen from the German perspective. The protagonist, Captain Hardt (Conrad Veidt), is a U-boat captain sent on a spying mission in 1917 to the Orkney Islands, there to liaise with a German female spy undercover as a school teacher, who has suborned a dissatisfied British naval officer to reveal the sailing times of the Grand Fleet in Scapa Flow.

The Spy in Black has only a few scenes on Hardt's U-boat, but they count. On a brief return to his submarine he brings some precious butter to a crew long starved of it. It is openly acknowledged that Hardt's mission as a U-boat captain is to destroy Britain's merchant shipping and thereby starve the country into submission, but early scenes in Berlin of him and his officers being unable to get good food even at expensive restaurants stress that privation cut both ways. After he is double-crossed, Hardt takes over a merchant ship with the help of German POWs only to be torpedoed by his own U-boat, which is then sunk by a British destroyer. He remains honourable to the end, refusing to abandon ship and going to his death in his submarine commander's uniform, an officer, not a spy.

The plea to recognize one's wartime enemies as human was ill timed. On 9 September 1939, just 22 days after *The Spy in Black* was released in UK cinemas, Britain declared war on Germany for its invasion of Poland. Learning the lessons of the First World War, it sent its merchant ships in large convoys from the outset. But Britain's pre-war naval strategy – to nullify the threat of the U-boats by confining them to their North Sea and Baltic bases – was undermined by the swift German conquest of France, which meant the *Kriegsmarine* could use French Atlantic ports as U-boat bases. During 1940–41, a period U-boat captains called the 'Happy Time', they ranged at will in the Atlantic sea lanes. Churchill later confessed that the only thing he had truly feared in the Second World War, as in the First, was the threat to Britain's survival posed by U-boats.

The ensuing 'Battle of the Atlantic' was the pivot of the early years of the war. With Britain importing two-thirds of its food and 95 per cent of its petrol, it was only the relatively small number of U-boats (in 1939 Germany had only 43 in operation) that kept Britain from collapse.[8] Aside from improved diesel-electric engines, Germany's new U-boats were little altered from those of the First World War. The standard model, the Type VII, had a crew of four officers and 44 ratings. At 10 knots it could cover a distance of nearly 15,000 kilometres (8,000 mi.), carry fourteen torpedoes, crash-dive in thirty seconds and, when submerged, work on electric motors. A 'wolf pack' of these Type VII U-boats could devastate an enemy supply convoy very quickly.

Although the Type VII was the standard U-boat design for the Second World War, in the last two years of the war Germany produced 118 of the more advanced Type XXI U-boats. The Type XXI was a radical prototype, the first submarine designed to operate primarily when submerged rather than as a surface vessel that could submerge only for brief periods. Had Germany had these numbers of the Type XXI in 1939, the course of the war might have been very different.

Len Deighton's bracingly iconoclastic history of the Second World War describes the conditions for the crews of both German and British submarines:

> There were no bathing facilities, and only one lavatory which could not be used when the submarine dived. When under attack the lavatory might well be out of action for 24 hours. No-one shaved and most didn't change even one article of clothing for the entire voyage. The stink of human bodies was mixed with those of oil and fuel. There was also the pervading smell of mould, for in the damp air everything, from bread to log books, went mouldy. The men – mostly young, for only young men could endure the hardships and the stress – were apt to douse themselves in eau de cologne to exchange one smell for another.[9]

Very little of this noxious reality made its way into films about submarine warfare, although novels such as *Surface!* and *Das Boot* were more brutally frank.

One of the first casualties of war was the 1930 London Naval Treaty, which had stipulated that submarines could not sink merchant vessels until passengers and crew were off-boarded and safe, meaning that land was within sailing distance by lifeboats. Yet just twelve hours after the declaration of war *U-30* sighted and torpedoed a passenger liner, which had departed Liverpool before the outbreak of war, off the coast of

Donegal. One hundred and twelve people died. Shortly afterwards, in November 1939, the commander-in-chief of U-boats issued Standing Order 154, which instructed:

> Rescue no-one and take no-one aboard. Do not concern yourselves with the ship's boats. Weather conditions and the proximity of land are of no account . . . The enemy started this war in order to destroy us, and thus nothing else matters.[10]

The moral burden for the breaking of the 1930 Naval Treaty and for unleashing USW is still contested. Alan Bleasdale's powerful TV drama *The Sinking of the Laconia* (2012) examines an incident in September 1942 when the British troopship *Laconia* was torpedoed and sunk by U-boat *U-156*, 100 kilometres (600 mi.) off the west coast of Africa. Upon realizing the survivors included civilians and Italian POWs, *U-156*'s captain, Werner Hartenstein, ordered that some be taken on board, while others in lifeboats were provided with food and water. He informed the Allies that he was protecting survivors and that until they were picked up he would not engage in hostile action. Despite this, American bombers attacked the surfaced *U-156*, killing some of the crew and survivors, forcing the submarine to leave the survivors to be picked up later.

As a result of the incident Admiral Donitz issued the 'Laconia Order' expressly forbidding actions such as Hartenstein's. But Bleasdale's portrayal of Donitz as a decent but conflicted man forced reluctantly to forbid rescue efforts by his submarine crews does not square with history. Donitz was a dedicated fascist and the man who issued Standing Order 154 in 1939, three years before the Laconia Order. It was that order that Hartenstein ignored. The Laconia Order simply restated it to ensure such things would not recur. Unlike Bleasdale's excellent *The Monocled Mutineer* (1984), *The Sinking of the Laconia* revises a history that does not need revision.

The interwar period had produced major advances in anti-submarine technology. The Royal Navy's Anti-Submarine Establishment led the way in the creation of ASW, most particularly the creation of what would become known as sonar (**So**und **Na**vigation **R**anging) but was at the time known as ASDIC after the body that created it, the Allied Submarine Detection Investigation Committee. ASDIC projected a pulse of sound – a 'ping' – which, upon hitting another object, reflected a pulse back. The time between sending and receiving indicated the distance of the object.

British tracking of U-boat movements was undertaken by the Admiralty's Submarine Tracking Room, based in the 'Citadel' adjacent to the Admiralty on Trafalgar Square.[11] The STR used High Frequency Direction Finding (HF/DF, or 'Huff Duff'), radio fixes and sightings to triangulate a U-boat's location, but however accurate these were, they could not confirm its direction of travel. This all changed with the cracking of Germany's Enigma coding machine, which until 1941 produced so many variations that its codes were simply impossible to decipher.

The breakthrough occurred in May 1941 when the British cruiser HMS *Bulldog* forced *U-110* to the surface. Boarding the U-boat, British sailors discovered an intact Enigma machine, along with its codebooks, rotor settings for the next three months and the key to the 'Hydra' Enigma code for the rest of the war. In October 1942 three sailors from another British cruiser boarded the stricken *U-559*, where they retrieved and removed the codes for the 'Shark' Enigma code, the most complex of all, before the submarine sank, drowning two of them.[12]

The American film *U-571* (2000) used the retrieval of the Enigma machine from a German submarine as the basis of its story, but changed the narrative so this is achieved by a small party of heroic American submariners on a covert mission to board the fictional *U-571* and after several hair-raising incidents bring it safely back to the Allies. This switch, deemed necessary for its domestic audience, has obscured *U-571*'s considerable qualities as a taut, well-constructed adventure film. Ever eager to play to the gallery, British prime minister Tony Blair called *U-571* an 'affront' to the British sailors who had actually retrieved the

Enigma machine, but the film's bigger anachronism was its choice of enemy. The real focus of American submarine operations in the Second World War was not Germany but Japan.

From its first version, drafted in 1897, the U.S. Department of Defense had regularly updated 'War Plan Orange', America's overall military strategy for a possible war with Japan. Japan's submarine fleet was born in 1904 when it bought five Holland-type submarines from the Electric Boat Company. After the First World War Japan's geo-strategic ambitions in the Pacific and Asian theatres expanded significantly. By 1931 the Imperial Japanese Navy (IJN) had a total of 72 submarines, some of which saw action off the Chinese coast in the Sino-Japanese War in 1937. In December 1941 two dozen IJN submarines were in the vanguard of the surprise attack on Pearl Harbor. A few days later Japanese submarines were patrolling off the American west coast.

The year 1941 was the zenith of Japan's ambition to create a 'Greater East-Asia Co-Prosperity Sphere' in the Pacific under Japan's rule. Before Pearl Harbor, Admiral Yamamoto had warned his superiors that while

First submarine of the Imperial Japanese Navy (*Holland 1*-class), 1904, purchased from the United States during the Russo-Japanese War.

he could guarantee an initial victory he could not do the same in the years after. Pearl Harbor was, in any case, a pyrrhic victory. Many of the U.S. Pacific Fleet's destroyers were at sea at the time of the attack, while those that were damaged sank in shallow waters and were quickly raised. Just two hours after the attack, Admiral Hart, Commander of the U.S. Asiatic Fleet, sent a message to his ships –'Execute unrestricted air and submarine warfare against Japan.' He made clear that *all* Japanese shipping (military, merchant or civilian) was fair game and should be sunk without warning. International law was void and did not apply.[13]

Japan's forces were too far extended from a homeland even more vulnerable to food shortages than Britain. The *Kriegsmarine* urged the IJN to concentrate its efforts on sinking U.S. merchant shipping but the Japanese ignored the advice, instead prioritizing American battleships and aircraft carriers. IJN submarine captains were even forbidden from torpedoing merchant shipping if they had been ordered to target specific U.S. Navy vessels. It was not long before the tide turned.

The Battle of Midway in June 1942 dealt the IJN a devastating blow from which it never recovered. From this point U.S. submarines moved into the Pacific in force. They adopted the *Kriegsmarine* strategy of operating in 'wolf packs' – that is, large numbers of submarines surrounding a victim, like a Japanese aircraft carrier – and finishing it off. In 1944 U.S. submarines destroyed seven Japanese aircraft carriers as well as the battleship *Kongo*. By August 1945, when Japan surrendered after atomic bombs were dropped on Hiroshima and Nagasaki, U.S. submarines had sunk 1,300 Japanese merchant ships, three-fifths of its entire merchant fleet, and roughly two hundred Japanese warships.

America's victory over Japan had been inevitable from the start. Big battalions always win. But it was still necessary, for the benefit of civilian morale, that U.S. submarine operations in the Pacific be repackaged in a conventionally heroic mode. How this was achieved is examined in Matthew McGrew's academic study of 2011, 'Beneath the Surface: American Culture and Submarine Warfare in the Twentieth Century'. McGrew's work is a scrupulous analysis but its central contention – that cultural perceptions of the submarine guided and directed their use during the twentieth century; that, in his words, 'discourse led strategy' – is in my view overstated.[14]

The clearest example of discourse in the submarine genre is the extent to which British and American films produced during the war faithfully reflected the needs of state propaganda and arguments about justifiable retaliation. *Destination Tokyo* (dir. Delmer Daves, 1943), a big-budget Hollywood production starring Cary Grant, not only whitewashed the nature of USW in the Pacific but dramatized an actual U.S. military operation, 'the Doolittle Raid', the first airstrike by U.S. airforces against Tokyo. This operation acted both as retribution for Pearl Harbor and a signal that the USA could and would bring the war to the Japanese mainland.

In the film the submarine USS *Copperfin* must sail through dangerous coastal defences into Tokyo Bay, land a reconnaissance team to obtain crucial meteorological information, and then pick them up to relay that information back to the waiting bombers. The submarine is thus presented as a crucial component of an important land-based attack, a role it seldom played in reality.

USS *Tang* off the Mare Island Navy Yard, California, December 1943.

Crewmen from
drowned aircrafts
taken aboard
USS *Tang* near the
Pacific island of Truk
(now Chuuk Lagoon),
May 1944.

Destination Tokyo is a revealing snapshot, taken in the midst of the war against Japan, of America's attitude towards its enemy. Its only genuine comparator is the classic British film *We Dive at Dawn* (dir. Anthony Asquith, 1943), which is equally careful to establish its characters as versions of an everyman. Early scenes of the crew of HMS *Sea Tiger* on shore leave dip into working-class life – urban backstreets, terraced houses and pubs – for a brief tapestry of the crew's civilian lives. This done, the film pulls the audience in to the *Sea Tiger*'s mission to find and sink the German destroyer *Brandenburg* in the Baltic Sea before it can reach the safety of the Kiel Canal.

Most of the film, aside from an on-shore detour in Denmark for some conventional heroics, is a narrative of grim professionalism. The *Sea Tiger*'s slow passage through a minefield in the Baltic straits is punctuated by the captain's staccato orders to the engine room to continuously alter depth and speed. The film's digression to land only serves to pull attention away from the real focus of British submarine warfare at the time, the grim Battle of the Atlantic, in which submarine crews did not leave their boats to infiltrate German bases in the manner of elite commandos.

Sinking of the Japanese destroyer *Yamakaze* as seen from the periscope of the American submarine USS *Nautilus*, June 1942.

It was not until the 1950s and '60s that the submarine genre found its settled form. Between 1951 and 1965 there were at least eighteen popular films produced for a mass audience that focused on submarines in the Second World War alone (there were many other submarine movies with contemporary themes). These films were mostly Hollywood productions but they included the Swedish *Ubat 39* (dir. Hampe Faustman, 1952), the Polish *Orzel* (dir. Leonard Buczkowski, 1959) and the Italian *La grande speranza* (dir. Duilio Coletti, 1965). The prime example of the genre is *Run Silent, Run Deep* (1957), directed by Robert Wise, which many regard as the quintessential submarine film.

It was no coincidence that at a time when the USA was launching its first nuclear-powered submarines, its cinema industry was presenting the American submarine and its crew as defenders of democracy against a totalitarian foe. An early example, *Operation Pacific* (dir. George Waggner, 1951), had done so with simplistic fervour, with John Wayne's U.S. submarine *Thunderfish* roaming the Pacific rescuing children and nuns from the advancing Japanese, stopping only to

Life onboard USS *Cuttlefish* while in the Pacific, June 1943.

torpedo the occasional aircraft carrier. At no point does it hunt with a wolf pack.

So long as a submarine film conformed to the requirements of state propaganda, the U.S. military was glad to assist with its production. For *Run Silent, Run Deep* the U.S. Navy allowed the submarine USS *Redfish* to be used for exterior shots and a serving submarine captain was seconded as technical advisor. The film already had a high level of technical accuracy, as it was based on a novel by Edward L. Beach, who had commanded U.S. submarines during the Second World War. Beach went on to serve as Naval Aide to President Eisenhower from 1953 to 1957 and then as commander of the nuclear submarine USS *Triton*, which in 1960 completed an unprecedented 84-day circumnavigation of Earth without surfacing.

Taking pains to establish a credible Second World War submarine environment and reasonably complex characters, Beach's novel is regarded by aficionados of the genre as 'the Holy Grail of submarine novels . . . the one everyone who comes later has to live up to'.[15] However, the film adaptation departed greatly from its source material, preferring to invert the core of the plot, in which a seasoned captain has to mentor a green XO and crew, to create instead a modern *Moby Dick* for the submarine service.

The film's Ahab is Captain Richardson (Clark Gable), a man obsessed with sinking the Japanese destroyer *Akikaze*, commanded by the notorious 'Bungo Pete', which destroyed his last submarine. In pursuing his vendetta he butts heads with his new submarine's XO Commander Bledsoe (Burt Lancaster), who had expected to assume command of USS *Nerka* and who considers Richardson unsuitable for command.

It is clear from the start of the mission that Richardson intends to disobey orders and head to the dangerous Bungo Straits to sink the *Akikaze*. In preparation for his revenge duel, he hoards torpedoes that could be used against other ships and has the crew practise 'bow shots' (firing from aft) and crash diving at record speeds. At the climax of the film, when it is discovered that it is not the *Akikaze* that was responsible for the sinking of u.s. ships but a Japanese submarine that used it as cover, Richardson is mortally injured and Bledsoe leads a crew whose nerves are already stretched to breaking point.

Run Silent, Run Deep set a benchmark for submarine films. Unusually for the late 1950s it was filmed in black-and-white, a decision that works in its favour by adding a patina of 1940s wartime atmosphere to a film revelling in every trope of the submarine genre. Wise had the cast train with real submariners to ensure they knew and could fluently perform torpedo-firing procedures such as range and bearing calculations. The attack scenes were regarded by serving submariners as unusually accurate and realistic, and to this day provide a glimpse of how a u.s. submarine tracked and attacked Japanese shipping during the Second World War.

Run Silent, Run Deep also acknowledged that it was the basic mission of u.s. submarines to wage usw against merchant shipping, a sign that by 1957 the usa was self-confident enough to admit it had used whatever means were necessary to defeat the Japanese. Other American Second World War submarine films of the era are either pale copies or eager competitors. *Hellcats of the Navy* (dir. Nathan Juran, 1957), *The Enemy Below* (dir. Dick Powell, 1957) and *Torpedo Run* (dir. Joseph Pevney, 1958) are all solid efforts but add little to the genre, in terms of either content or technique.

It was not until 1981 that a film based around submarine warfare in the Second World War challenged and redefined the entire genre. *Das Boot* (dir. Wolfgang Petersen, 1981, extended director's edition 1997), based on the 1973 novel by Lothar-Günther Buchheim, is by some distance the gold standard of the submarine film. Buchheim's original novel remains the genre's only credible contender for a permanent place among the masterpieces of world literature.

Buchheim's novel is born of his time as a young war correspondent with the *Kriegsmarine*, writing about his experiences on German destroyers and submarines, in particular a six-week patrol with U-boat

U-96 in the Atlantic in 1941 which left permanent psychological scars. *Das Boot* tells
the story of a patrol by the fictional *U-A*
departing La Rochelle naval base with orders
to sink as much merchant shipping as possible. Despite its savagely ironic ending,
the patrol is in many respects routine – in
the same sense that Ivan Denisovich's day
in the Gulag is a routine one.

Like all U-boats, the *U-A* experiences
long periods of inactivity and appalling
living conditions, punctuated by bursts of
action as it tries (usually without success) to
find and sink a convoy ship. Buchheim's
genius is in granular detail – the rancid smell
of oil and farts inside the vessel, nagging
obsession with a trapped fly or a comrade's
peeling skin, how to use the head without
blowback, men pissing overboard from the
conning tower, men freezing on the conning tower, the exact means
of slicing and eating lemons, having a celebratory beer after sinking a
ship, reading books falling apart from damp and mould, eating bread
falling apart from damp and mould, and much more. No other novel
of life on a submarine comes anywhere near *Das Boot*'s level of
immersive reality.

Poster for *Run Silent,
Run Deep* (dir.
Robert Wise, 1958).

Buchheim was an art collector who after the war established his
own publishing house and gallery. His visual sensitivity feeds exquisite
depictions of the sea's rhythm and turmoil. He has a precise command
of colour which he brings to observations from the conning tower.

> I went on the bridge as often as I could. The sky was a different
> colour each morning. There were skies of vitriol and pistachio
> green, skies astringent green as lime juice held to the light, or

dull as the greenish froth from a boiled over saucepan of spinach, or ice cold as a cobalt green shading to Naples yellow.

At one point he plays with red alone:

> The reds seemed to be the richest and most varied shades of all, ranging from a faint pink flush to delicate opaline rose, from hazy mallow-red to harsh hydrant-red. Between these lay mother-of-pearl red, geranium red and scarlet, and between red and yellow lay infinite gradations of orange.[16]

Buchheim paints in prose, but his real descriptive power is in summoning the sheer physicality of rain, storm and wave. When the narrator, a war correspondent assigned to the boat, is taking bridge duty, a heavy rainstorm suddenly descends:

> Torrents and rain and salvoes of spray met and mingled on our faces. The deluge seemed to descend on us from some gargantuan bucket. The white-veined glassy green of the waves vanished. Not a glimmer, not a hint of colour. Nothing but uniform, soul destroying grey . . . The lookouts stood like monoliths defying a primeval flood. Binoculars were useless – they would have blurred in seconds.[17]

In a risky narrative stroke, Buchheim begins the novel with a long segment of maddening boredom (for the crew) conjured with hypnotic literary skill. After the *U-A* finally torpedoes a merchantman, it is pursued relentlessly by a British destroyer for several days in a non-stop barrage of depth charges that almost destroys the submarine and calls for maximum effort from the crew to hold it and themselves together. Later, in one of the most painfully elongated passages of the novel, the *U-A* is battered for weeks on end by a relentless storm, with no respite except for the one or two hours it submerges to let the crew eat.

Buchheim's novel was a literary sensation when first published, selling 3 million copies in Germany alone. Translated into eighteen languages, it became an international best-seller. Not all reviewers appreciated Buchheim's intention to tell an honest story of ordinary men trapped in appalling circumstances and surviving as best they could. Condemning what it called Buchheim's 'bid to soften history's judgement on 40,000 men who volunteered to wage total war on civilians and were themselves almost totally destroyed', the *New York Times* review in 1981 celebrated '30,000 of them dying the terrible deaths they richly deserved'.

Wolfgang Petersen's faithful film adaptation of Buchheim's novel simply ignored these enmities. Like its source material, it honours the basic humanity of the U-boat crew by focusing on their routine concerns, petty gossip, scatological humour and agonizing boredom. Although it rarely touches on ideological concerns, it makes clear that most of the crew, especially the veteran captain, have little respect for fascist and German state propaganda. Above all, Petersen's film creates a new way of experiencing the submarine. The director's use of hand-held cameras to leap through hatchways and compartments with the crew as they rush to battle stations, although now a familiar part of the genre, were revolutionary at the time. The enclosed set, built to U-boat Type VII specifications, supplemented by intense close-ups, serve to lock the viewer inside the vessel with a crew that is hot, tired, unshaven, sweating and afraid. When the depth charges come they are sudden, demonic, intense flashes of crashing orange, searing the viewer's eyes as the crew is battered to breaking point.

Das Boot stood alone. In the 1980s the submarine genre rejected psychology and humanism for Reaganite ideology, with lamentable results for its overall quality. Until then its premier novelists had been the British authors Douglas Reeman and Alexander Fullerton. With the arguable exception of Sven Hassel, whose cynical tales of a panzer regiment in the Second World War have enduring macho appeal, Reeman is the pre-eminent popular novelist of that war. Although both

The most talked about movie in Germany is coming to America. **Das Boot**

The other side of World War II.

Hitler sent out 40,000 men aboard German U boats during World War II. Less than 10,000 returned. This is the story of 42 raw recruits caught up in a war they didn't understand, and the Captain who must lead them in their struggle to survive.

Poster for *Das Boot* (dir. Wolfgang Petersen, 1981).

Reeman and Fullerton produced too many novels, which trailed off in quality towards the end of their long careers, their best works possess a quiet style and emotional subtlety totally absent from the modern military techno-thriller.

Reeman's nearest equivalent to *Das Boot*, the superb *With Blood and Iron* (1964), tells the story of the last mission of German U-boat captain Rudolf Steiger in 1944. Expertly capturing the social complexities of German–French relations in occupied France, the novel also presents several visceral action set pieces, such as when Steiger's submarine accidentally surfaces in the midst of an Allied flotilla and must then fight desperately for its life.

Steiger appears the quintessential Nazi commander, dedicated and ruthless, but throughout the story his outer and inner defences crumble. By the end he doubts the rightness of his cause and his own rectitude. Rather than implode in self-destruction, he re-evaluates and sees the possibility of a new life when, at the close, his submarine is sunk and he is taken prisoner. His crew is also exceptionally well drawn, with more backstory than is given to Buchheim's. One of the secondary characters, Gunner Max Konig, is an ex-Communist who has taken on a seaman's identity and signed up for Steiger's submarine. Through him we see a perspective on the Third Reich not often considered, that of the anti-Nazi German keeping his head down and trying to survive until better days.

Although he rarely equals the beauty of Buchheim's descriptive prose, Reeman is a skilled literary craftsman with tight control of character and plot. His later major novel of submarine warfare in the Second World War, *Strike from the Sea* (1978), follows the mission of British

submariners assuming command of 'the world's largest and most dangerous submarine', the French *Soufrière* (based on the Free French
Cruiser Submarine *Surcouf*, which until her sinking in 1942 was the
largest submarine ever built) in Indo-China and using it to defend
Singapore. Yet something is missing. *Strike from the Sea* is a skilful and
gripping thriller but it lacks *With Blood and Iron*'s heightened
intensity.

Reeman's nearest competitor, Alexander Fullerton, never bettered
his outstanding debut, *Surface!* (1953), a novel which shares some of *Das
Boot*'s ability to capture the quotidian reality of life in a Second World
War submarine, HMS *Seahound*, assigned to patrol the coast of Japan
after the defeat of Germany. Although there is a perfunctory mission,
the landing of some British commandos, the focus of the book is on the
men of the *Seahound* and the conditions they endure as the submarine
waits on the seabed to deliver its cargo. Most of the book concerns the
worries of the crew about how they will adjust to post-war life.

Das Boot (1981, dir.
Wolfgang Petersen).

Surface! was based on Fullerton's wartime service with the British submarine HMS *Seadog* in the Pacific and received both critical and popular acclaim. In addition to the Everard series Fullerton wrote 34 novels on naval warfare, but his later books suffer from the lack of personal motivation to memorialize his comrades that so animated *Surface!*. Further novels by Fullerton centring on British submarines in the Second World War, such as *The Waiting Game* (1961), *A Share of Honour* (1982) and *Submariner* (2008), are solid entertainments but far too easily achieved.

Fullerton and Reeman went to the well too often for their own good, one reason why the naval fictions of Nicholas Monsarrat and Alistair MacLean have outlasted them. Monsarrat's *The Cruel Sea* (1951) and MacLean's *HMS Ulysses* (1955) are brutal narratives of Britain's Arctic convoys to Soviet Russia. In these books the German submarine is an invisible, sadistic monster relentlessly torturing British seamen, leaving their nerves frayed and courage eroded. This mirrored the harrowing reality of the Arctic convoys, demonstrated in June 1942 when an entire 24-merchant-ship convoy heading for Murmansk was methodically annihilated by combined U-boat and Luftwaffe attack. Such was the deep remembrance of the Arctic convoys' ordeals that Buchheim, when seeking to rehabilitate the U-boat crew, set his novel in the wide Atlantic and not the North Sea route to Russia.

The conventional account of submarine warfare in the Second World War was crafted by the victors and was, inevitably, one-sided. For three decades after 1945 it sank deep into the collective psyche of the victorious nations, not simply via Anglo-American films but also through the influence of children's stories, comics and popular novels. Nostalgic commemoration of Britain's role in the Second World War expanded in proportion to its declining power and status in the world. From the 'Finest Hour' to the 'Desert Rats' to the 'Chindits', a stirring tapestry of heroism against the odds unfolded for audiences young and old, a balm and salve to a country still beset by rationing in the 1950s and humiliated at Suez in 1956.

Films such as *The Battle of the River Plate*, *The Colditz Story*, *Reach for the Sky*, *The Dam Busters* and *Dunkirk* reassured the British that theirs was a noble cause fought nobly. It was a powerful narrative precisely because of its core of truth. The visual graphic at the beginning of the popular British sitcom *Dad's Army* of British retreat in 1940 is played for laughs ('Who do you think you are kidding, Mr Hitler, if you think we're on the run?') but is also strategically exact. Nazi armies did close in on the UK and it did refuse to surrender. In the 1950s a plethora of quietly stirring narratives such as Edward Young's classic *One of Our Submarines* (1952), a memoir of his command of HMS *Storm* from 1942 to 1945 in the North Sea and the Indian Ocean, cemented this history in the public mind.

The mythologized history of the Second World War, of a time when Britain 'stood alone' against Nazi invasion, has not yet lost its potency. On the contrary, Brexit has boosted it still further, although it has replaced an original core of noble anti-fascism with a sullen English nationalism. Regardless, the struggle at sea remains emblematic. In *Authentocrats* (2018), Joe Kennedy tells of childhood visits in the 1990s to a museum in North Yorkshire called Eden Camp, a former POW camp whose Nissan huts had been refitted to play out different aspects of the war. He vividly recalls that, 'The most haunting display was an imitation U-boat with a soundtrack of incessant sonar pings, which, flaunting its poetic license, had portholes so visitors could see dummies dressed up to look like drowned merchant mariners "floating" past.'[18]

The UK is not the only country to retrofit history to make a contemporary point. India's first submarine film *The Ghazi Attack* (dir. Sankalp Reddy, 2017) – set just before the outbreak of the Indo-Pakistani War of 1971, when Pakistan and India went to war after East Pakistan broke away to form Bangladesh – is not far removed from a *Commando* comic. The film is based on the 'true' story of the sinking of the Pakistani Navy's flagship submarine, PNS *Ghazi*, by the Indian diesel-electric submarine INS *Iranj*, seemingly because the *Ghazi* was on the verge of launching missiles at India's naval base at Visakhapatnam Port (aka Visag).

In reality the *Ghazi* was probably sunk not by submarine but by the Indian destroyer INS *Rajput*. The film conflates this with an incident during the war in which a Pakistani submarine, PNS *Hangor*, fired upon and sank an Indian frigate, INS *Khukri*. The *Khukri* was the first ship sunk in action by a submarine since the Second World War. While India's navy easily defeated Pakistan's in 1971, the *Hangor*'s successful strike at one of its ships hurt India's national pride and produced a version of history, 46 years later, that inverted the sinking by making the *Hangor* an Indian submarine, and one that struck first.

Although the exact sequence of events in 1971 remains contested (and *The Ghazi Attack* does not untangle them), the film has immense fascination as a first foray by the Indian film industry into the traditional submarine genre. Frothing with melodramatic nationalism, it adapts the entire range of the genre's clichés to an emotive Bollywood style. Hence we have the authoritarian Captain Singh (Kay Kay Menon) butting heads with his XO Lieutenant Commander Varma (Rana Daggubati). When Singh ignores orders not to fire on Pakistani vessels unless first fired upon, Varma insists on correct procedure, whereupon the captain pulls a gun on him. The two officers are reconciled once the *Iranj* is itself attacked, before the captain is killed and the XO steps up to assume the burdens of command.

The Pakistani enemy is epitomized by the glowering *Ghazi* captain Razak. 'It's not over until we wipe Visag from the map,' he tells his crew, bolstering them after a setback. 'Long live Pakistan!' he yells, shaking his fist. 'Long live Pakistan!' they reply in unison. Later, when the *Iranj*, torpedoed and seemingly defeated, taunts the *Ghazi*, its entire crew singing the Indian national anthem to goad the Pakistani sub into firing on them and thus revealing its position, Razak is driven to distraction. 'Damn Indians!' he spits venomously. 'The British were right about them!'

Even modern video games honour the conventional mythology of the Second World War. But while *Call of Duty* and other first-person shooters prefer black ops or Navy SEALs scenarios, submarine games offer simulation and strategy rather than blunt-force violence. Popular submarine sims such as *Silent Service* (1985), *Silent Hunter III* (2005) and *Silent Hunter 4: Wolves of the Pacific* (2007) provide a realistic facsimile of command under stress instead of a fantasy of death-dealing heroism from behind an AR-15 assault rifle. Many focus on German U-boats or Allied submarines fighting the Battle of the Atlantic.

As the submarine is and has always been primarily a military vessel, it is unsurprising that its portrayal in popular fiction is dominated by tales of warfare. These are common themes in human culture. The war story, in all its forms, has been a staple of popular mythology from the Trojan War to the Iraq War, from Homer to *Black Hawk Down*. The fealty of modern sub sims and an Indian film made seventy years after the end of the Second World War to the cinematic tropes derived from that conflict demonstrates that it remains central to the image of the submarine in popular culture. It is the crucible through which the submarine emerged as something immediately recognizable in film, literature, comics and computer games, resonant with its own distinctive aesthetic and style, a claustrophobic hothouse of periscopes, sonar, torpedoes, depth charges and a crew pushed to extremes.

The submarine genre fits awkwardly within the conventional war story. Part of the reason for this is the nature of submarine activity in the two world wars, which was essentially that of unrestricted submarine warfare (USW): that is, attacking and sinking civilian and merchant vessels without warning. Contrary to popular myth, rarely does a submarine engage another submarine. The problems this presents for the depiction of the submarine and its crew in war fiction and war propaganda requires a variety of diversionary strategies that dominate the genre.

The classic triad of the Armed Forces – Army, Navy and Air Force – are notorious for their institutionalization of social class. 'Officers and men' is accepted code for middle-class and working-class. In particular, air force pilots and naval officers are signified for what they invariably are – polished products of social and educational privilege,

Second World War recruitment poster for the u.s. Submarine Force, c. 1944.

loyal representatives of their country's ruling class supported by sturdy artisans working in radar, sonar, maintenance or engineering. The Army, as the biggest and most heterogeneous force, contains a more complex set of representations. Because of the Army's closer relationship to direct physical violence, it is allowed that working-class subordinates – NCOs, elite commandos and so on – have their place and occasionally their dignity, as useful tools of upper-class strategists.

Based on the experiences of large bodies of working-class men conscripted into the armed forces to defeat the threat of militaristic fascism, the post-1945 era saw a great expansion of the literary war story. These strayed far beyond tales of career officers unquestioningly carrying out the foreign policy of their government. In particular, American novels such as *The Naked and the Dead* (1948), *From Here to Eternity* (1951) and *The Thin Red Line* (1962) focused on the morally problematic nature of war and combat, with enlisted men and NCOs as protagonists.

These novels centre on the army, leaving the navy and air force in the safer hands of the middle-class officer. In similar fashion, the populist appeal of the submarine genre derives from the submarine service's relative autonomy from the rigid class structure of the main services, from whom it has a radically different image, style and mystique. In a submarine officers and ratings work in far closer personal proximity, almost intimacy. In the older diesel-electric submarines the captain was the only person with his own (tiny) cabin. All ranks would share the same toilet. Even in modern nuclear-powered submarines only the captain and the executive officer (XO) get their own head. Other officers share with the ratings.

The submarine's unrelenting focus on technology, science and engineering (batteries, oil, pipes, sonar, water tanks) stresses routine industry and labour far more than the other, more traditional services. Of the U.S. Navy's nuclear submarine training programme, a retired USN officer explained:

> Submarine School is your crash course in how to drive a sub, sonar, contact tracking, damage control, flooding response, fire-fighting, weapon systems. Everyone on board is trained to fight flooding. Everyone is an amateur firefighter. Everyone onboard is trained on the basics of every system onboard. Even a cook knows how fission works.[19]

The unique conditions shared by submarine crews are specifically invoked in the 2018 film *Hunter Killer* (dir. Donovan Marsh), in which the U.S. submarine captain makes an explicit plea to his Russian counterpart when needing his assistance. 'We're not enemies, we're brothers. Who else understands what we go through down here?' he asks, suggesting that submariners feel more kinship with enemy submariners than with their surface-based commanding officers and their compatriots in the other armed services, let alone in civilian life.

2

THE SUBMARINE IN POLITICS

If warfare is the continuation of politics by other means, then the use of the submarine in war, or in strategies intended to threaten, prevent or curtail war, is a political statement. Often that statement is crude. Since the First World War levels of fire-power and ease of deployment have been vital to the strategic value of the submarine, but often the simple *number* of submarines a country possesses is an indicator, however irrational, of superpower status.

By 2021 China's submarine fleet technically exceeded that of the USA (79 to 68), although the story told by numbers alone is deceptive. The U.S. fleet contains more nuclear-powered submarines than China's and is thus more mobile and lethal. Russia, at a total of 64, is not far behind its two main rivals for superpower status. Other countries are expanding their submarine fleets, some rapidly – North Korea (36, excluding a large number of small coastal submarines and midget-subs), Iran (29), South Korea (22), India (17) and Turkey (12) all boast of their growing submarine capacity in order to enhance their political and military status on the world stage.

At present the submarine fleets of those in the second division (with the exception of the UK and France, which both possess nuclear-powered vessels) are all diesel-electric rather than nuclear powered, but it is only a matter of time before those countries move into the first, nuclear-powered division. At least two of Israel's fleet of five submarines already possess air-independent propulsion systems and can launch nuclear missiles if required. In October 2020 North Korea boasted that it would shortly have the capacity to fire ballistic missiles from its newest diesel-electric submarine.

Peter Hennessy and James Jinks's *The Silent Service* (2016), the most recent and authoritative account of the post-war Royal Navy Submarine Service, tells us that, notwithstanding its actual status as a medium-range European power, 'the United Kingdom is girdled with the harbours, facilities, and research laboratories needed to keep the country at the top of the range of the world's submarine powers.'[1] This is mostly symbolic. As of 2022 the UK has only four ballistic missile submarines – Vanguard-class submarines carrying Trident missiles – and of those only one is ever on permanent patrol, while the others are in either routine or deep maintenance. Their existence is part of what the progressive think tank Open Democracy called the UK's 'imperial pretensions to police the world's oceans'.[2]

The submarine genre reflects these imperial pretensions and their relative success or failure. The romantic futurism Jules Verne successfully conjured around his hypothetical submarine, the *Nautilus*, was soon erased by an escalating international arms race and a wave of pre-war jingoism. A central element of that jingoism was the 'invasion literature' of the late Victorian and Edwardian era, inaugurated by George Chesney's *The Battle of Dorking* (1871) and cemented in the popular mind by later works such as William Le Queux's *The Great War in England* (1897) and Erskine Childers's *The Riddle of the Sands* (1903). From the 1890s these narratives often involved enemy submarines or submersibles in sneak attacks for which the British were unprepared. Verne himself added to the sense of escalating war fever in his 1896 novel *Facing the Flag*, which replaces the utopian internationalism of *Twenty Leagues Under the Sea* with clichéd patriotic propaganda.

In *Facing the Flag* the brilliant but unstable French scientist Thomas Roch, who has designed a fearsome weapon of mass destruction, the Fulgurator, is kidnapped from a North Carolina asylum by Caribbean pirates led by the ruthless Count d'Artigas. The pirates have advanced technology of their own and induce him to build his WMD for them. When the British send a prototype submarine, HMS *Sword*, to attack the pirate's island hideaway, Verne gives us the first submarine battle in modern fiction, the precursor of every submarine-themed 'techno-thriller' from Tom Clancy onwards. Only when *Sword* is destroyed does a multi-national naval force led by the French annihilate the pirate base and the menace of the Fulgurator.

Following in Verne's wake, the decades before the First World War produced many popular submarine-themed stories, the most success-ful of which were Frank R. Stockton's *The Great Stone of Sardis* (1898), Herbert Strang's *Lord of the Seas* (1908) and Max Pemberton's *Captain Black* (1911), all of which essayed submarines far in advance of contemporary technology. While Stockton's *Sardis* is an attempt at Wellsian science fiction set fifty years in the future, the majority of the fledging genre were crude war-scare stories designed to stir fear of the sinister and underhand submarine, a technology only then reaching broader public awareness.

Pemberton was the pivotal figure here, an influence on the mass mind as significant as Wells and Conan Doyle, not simply through his novels but through the immense cultural influence he possessed as the editor of the popular boys' magazine *Chums* and, later, as a director of Northcliffe Newspapers. His most popular work, *The Iron Pirate: A Plain Tale of Strange Happenings on the Sea* (1893), tells the story of the anarchist pirate Captain Black and his 'gas-driven Ironclad warship'.

The *Iron Pirate*'s sequel, *Captain Black*, was promoted in *The Bookman* magazine in 1911 as an even more intense and gripping yarn, in which Black is now in possession of 'an electric-driven submarine equipped with periscopes, electric projectors, liquid oxygen, gyroscopic compasses, and engines for dealing death on that vast and awful scale which one associates with the exploits of the invincible Captain'. Pemberton's large readership were by this stage well acquainted with the submarine threat, as he had used them in *The Giant's Gate* (1901) to spearhead a treacherous French invasion of Great Britain.

Conan Doyle briefly returned to the submarine in 1917 with his collection of Sherlock Holmes short stories *His Last Bow*, which included 'The Adventure of the Bruce-Partington Plans'. Written during the war, and thus with the benefit of hindsight about the crippling effect of the U-boats on British shipping, the story is set in 1895, when Holmes and Watson are still living at 221B Baker Street, unburdened by the distractions of Mrs Watson or the Edwardian age.

When a junior official at the Woolwich Arsenal is found murdered, Holmes is called in by his brother, Mycroft – who 'occasionally *is* the British government' – because the victim had taken the plans of the revolutionary 'Bruce-Partington submarine' out of the office with him on the evening of his murder, which then went missing. Were a foreign power to obtain them, the international balance of power could shift. 'The whole force of the State is at your back if you should need it,' Mycroft assures Holmes, but, of course, he does not. Holmes soon tracks down the corrupt senior official of the Submarine Department

Illustration of the main parts of a submarine, from A. Frederick Collins and Virgil D. Collins, *The Boys' Book of Submarines* (1917).

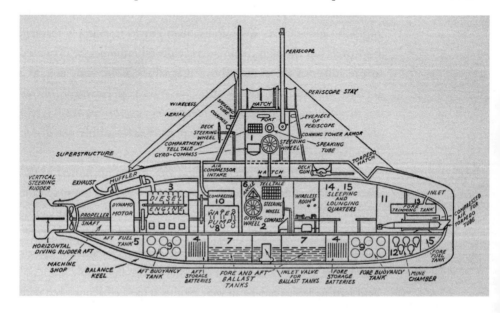

responsible for stealing the plans and sets a trap for the German spy to whom he is about to deliver them, retrieving them and thus safeguarding British submarine supremacy.[3]

Only after the Second World War, with the work of Douglas Reeman and Alexander Fullerton, did the submarine break out of the ghetto of marginal and escapist literature. His debut aside, Fullerton is best known for the nine-volume 'Mariner of England' series about his hero Nicholas Everard's naval adventures during the First World War (the first three volumes) and as an admiral during the Second World War (the later six volumes). The early trilogy includes *Patrol to the Golden Horn* (1978), in which a young Lieutenant Everard joins submarine *E-57* to complete a dangerous sabotage mission in Turkey at the very end of the war – Everard and explosives expert Burtenshaw must blow up the German battlecruiser *Goeben*, which guards the passage to the Black Sea.

The *Goeben* was a real German battlecruiser that had guarded the Golden Horn and propped up Germany's ally Turkey. The *E-57*'s mission is based on that of the *E-14*, which led to the loss of the submarine and the death of its crew.[4] Fullerton's great skill is not only to capture the mechanics of the submarine – of the laborious, endlessly repeated routine of adjusting ballast tanks, buoyancy; trim and depth – but to distil sensuous atmosphere and telling detail. From his own experience, he knew that on an extended submarine mission even officers would ignore dress codes. Thus the *E-57*'s captain wears 'old flannels with frayed turn-ups, and a cricket shirt that must once have been white but was now yellow with age. Tennis shoes. On patrol, nobody cared about uniform.'[5]

The *E-57*'s torturous passage through the Dardanelles, impassable to Allied submarines since the beginning of the war because of its dense chain of mines, is a masterly exercise in slowly building tension and dread. Two-thirds of the book are taken up with the passage. When the *E-57* reaches the Sea of Marmara and drops Everard and Burtenshaw outside Constantinople to liaise with the English spy 'The Grey Lady', the remainder becomes a conventional adventure, devoid of the clammy grip of the scenes on the submarine.

It is made clear to Everard that the sinking of the *Goeben* has little to do with defeating Germany but is designed to prevent it from falling into Turkish hands post-war, removing a possible obstacle to British passage through the Bosphorus to assist the White Russians in Crimea. 'First by action against *Goeben* as we now intend,' explains mission controller Commander Reaper, 'and in the longer term by establishing ourselves at the Horn and controlling the . . . well, for the time being let's just say the Bosphorus.'[6]

Fullerton wrote after historical distance had provided some objectivity about the long-term political strategies of all participants. In the 1920s and '30s the popular framing of submarine activity during the First World War was shaped entirely by patriotic sentiment. Germany, the defeated party, did not depict its submarine crews in the manner of British and American films, that is, as ruthless killers of civilians, indifferent to the rules of war and even basic human decency.

The issue of submarine warfare had festered throughout the 1920s. The extent to which relatively small numbers had posed an existential threat to powerful European states had come as a terrible shock. As the loser, Germany shouldered the blame. The 1919 Versailles Peace Treaty cited Germany's use of USW as one of the main reasons for imposing large war reparations on the country. While German nationalists and the political far right never accepted 'war guilt', and condemned the Versailles Treaty as unfair and punitive to Germany, the cultural elite of the Weimar Republic, drawn primarily from the liberal left, had no desire to inflame German militarism.

It therefore took until 1932 and the death rattle of Weimar for the German film industry to acknowledge its submarine service during the war. It was entirely fitting that the first film screened in Germany after Hitler became chancellor, on 2 February 1933, was the patriotic war movie *Morgenrot* (Red Dawn, dir. Vernon Sewell), a romantic defence of German U-boat warfare that contains no mention of torpedoing passenger liners, not even as a grim necessity. *Morgenrot* is a stirring anthem to martial valour, with its honourable U-boat captain willing

to go down with the boat in order to let his crew escape, and the crew preferring to die with him.

The London Naval Conference of 1930 was called to abolish or limit the size and number of submarines in the naval forces of the UK, France, the USA, Japan and Italy (under the terms of the Versailles Treaty, Germany was not allowed to build any submarines at all). The ensuing Naval Treaty, in addition to capping the signatories' total number of cruisers and destroyers, put upper limits on a submarine's displacement tonnage (its weight expressed in tons of water) and its range of armaments. It also, for the first time, placed submarines under the same international law that applied to surface vessels, a legal prohibition that vanished instantly upon outbreak of war in 1939.

The efforts of several naval conferences in the interwar years (Washington 1922, London 1930 and Geneva 1932) to restrict, if not abolish, submarine warfare, were doomed to failure by the refusal of leading powers to contemplate real disarmament. In 1931 Britain had 53 submarines, France 61, Italy 75, Japan 72 and the USA 81. After the First World War Germany had no submarines at all but it had secretly created a shell company based in the Netherlands, covertly funded by the German Navy, to safeguard its U-boat design plans and manufacturing expertise. It kept these skills current by building submarines for other countries.[7]

In 1930, during the London negotiations, Germany suggested that either other nations should disarm entirely to reach parity, or they should allow Germany to re-arm. The proposal was rejected. As a result, in 1932 the last German democratic government before Hitler's ascension to power approved a secret plan to begin building new U-boats. A year later the new Nazi regime accelerated the plan and *Morgenrot* played to packed cinemas. The Battle of the Atlantic was six years away.

It was only fitting, as the theme of the submarine had ushered in the Nazi regime, that it should play it out, in the provocative French film *Les Maudits* (The Damned, dir. René Clément, 1947). Set in the final days of the war, it centres on the occupants of a U-boat – senior Nazis, collaborators and a kidnapped French doctor – fleeing for South America. But these submariners have no future. Clément's film uses the submarine as a physical microcosm for an authoritarian society crumbling under its own internal stresses, with various ideologues and opportunists unable to either live with their failures or escape them. It also includes a reverse tracking shot through the cramped submarine that pre-dates Petersen's *Das Boot* by 45 years.

The transformation of the submarine film from a genre focused on military heroics to one concerned primarily with psychological strategy reflected the new era. After 1945, when a global 'hot war' ending in two bursts of nuclear fire was replaced by a more protracted and subtler cold one, the nature of the political terrain changed dramatically. Avoiding direct military engagement, the deployment of the respective power blocs' submarine fleets became a matter of strategic leverage in a complex political and ideological struggle.

In 1945 the Truman Proclamation extended the legal definition of American territory to include a 200-nautical-mile (370 km) Exclusive Economic Zone (EEZ) off the shores of the USA, including all the natural resources of its Continental Shelf. In the following decades other nations followed suit, creating EEZs across the globe. This eventually resulted in the UN Convention on the Law of the Sea, which replaced the older 'freedom of the sea' legal concept which had confined a nation's territorial rights to a limit of just 3 nautical miles (5.6 km) from its coastline.

At the same time, in February 1946, the U.S. Treasury asked the U.S. Embassy in Moscow to analyse Soviet geo-strategic intentions going forwards. Deputy Head of Mission George F. Kennan's 'Long Telegram' explained that, in Kennan's view, it was impossible for the USA and USSR to peacefully co-exist, as the nature of Soviet Communism meant the USSR would inevitably seek dominion over large parts of the world. Kennan therefore recommended a policy of 'Containment': a proxy battle across the globe using other countries as counters in the larger struggle between America and the Soviet Union. It was the foundational document of U.S. foreign policy in the post-war world.[8]

The Truman Proclamation and the Long Telegram effectively remapped the planet. In 1949 the U.S. Navy formed the top-secret Committee for Undersea Warfare specifically to research and develop ASW against Soviet submarines. As a result the SOSUS (**So**und **Su**rveillance **S**ystem) chain of underwater hydrophone arrays was installed on the ocean bed, carrying signals by undersea cables to onshore processing stations known as Evaluation Centers. SOSUS chains were located at key strategic locations, particularly the naval choke point between Greenland, Iceland and the UK known as the GUIK Gap, the only route into the North Atlantic for Soviet submarines departing their base on the Kola Peninsula. American and British Cold War naval strategy depended on policing and controlling this gap.[9]

One of the prime architects of this new world was U.S. Rear Admiral Hyman G. Rickover, who as director of the U.S. Navy's Naval Reactors Branch was the driving force behind the transition of its submarines from diesel-electric to nuclear powered (that is, powered from a pressurized water reactor). From 1958 until 1982 Rickover exercised an obsessive personal fiefdom over the U.S. Navy, personally interviewing and approving every prospective naval officer from junior ensigns to the commanders of nuclear-powered aircraft carriers. Presidents came and went but America's Cold War Navy, especially its submarine service in which he took a special interest, was Rickover's.

Rickover's most historic achievement was the development of the world's first nuclear-powered submarine, known as a Ship Submersible Nuclear (SSN). The contract for the first SSN was given to the modern incarnation of John Holland's Electric Boat Company. Since 1946 the Electric Boat Company had expanded and diversified into aircraft production in order to attract some of the Defense Department's enormous Cold War budget (between 1950 and 1953 America increased its overall defence spending from 5 per cent of GDP to 14 per cent). In 1952, having secured a large chunk of this budget, it rebranded itself as General Dynamics.

Portrait photograph of Rear Admiral Hyman G. Rickover, 1955.

In 1953 General Dynamics and the U.S. Navy launched SSN 571, aka USS *Nautilus*. This was the first submarine to be entirely air-independent, not needing to surface to take in air or expel fumes. Its nuclear reactor supplied enough power for life support, hot water and other functions for several months. In its first trial the *Nautilus* circumnavigated the globe without pause at a speed of 25 knots.

With the deployment of this one vessel the global balance of power shifted decisively. The *Nautilus* and the subsequent generation of U.S. nuclear-powered submarines could go deeper, move faster and further, and project force in wider theatres of war. In purely PR terms, its power derived not only from its unprecedented technological prowess and endurance at sea but from the deep associations of its name. A U.S.

Navy propaganda film of 1954 enthusiastically explained to American schools and cinema audiences, 'She is *Nautilus*, Queen of the Seas, and she and her sisters will keep those seas safe for freedom.'[10]

If the SSN was global warfare's John the Baptist, presaging the arrival of a force that would change the world, then the ship submersible ballistic nuclear (SSBN) was the Messiah, come not to bring peace but a sword. Both Japan and the Soviet Union had in the mid-1950s launched early prototype submarines capable of firing nuclear-tipped ballistic missiles, but neither of these were true SSBNs, as they were still diesel-electric powered and therefore had restricted range. The first fully operational SSBN in history, USS *George Washington*, was launched in June 1959 as part of Rickover's ever-expanding submarine fleet.

The *George Washington*, built as per Rickover's instructions by General Dynamics, was the first operational nuclear-powered multi-missile submarine fielded by any navy. In June 1960 it travelled from the General Dynamics facility at Groton, Connecticut, to Cape Canaveral, Florida, to load two Polaris Intercontinental Ballistic Missiles (ICBMs). After proceeding to the Atlantic Missile Test Range, on 20 July 1960 it successfully conducted the first Polaris missile launch from a submerged submarine. At 12:39 p.m. that day, the *George Washington*'s commanding officer telexed President Eisenhower: 'POLARIS–-FROM OUT OF THE DEEP TO TARGET. PERFECT.' The American Empire was born.

Others wished to emulate the USA, even if they had to ride on their coat-tails. In 1953, to coincide with the launch of the *Nautilus*, the USA and UK drew up the Emergency Joint U.S./UK Submarine War Plan, which divided the North Atlantic into American and British patrol zones. Two years after the 1958 Mutual Defence Agreement between the two countries, the UK launched its first SSN, HMS *Dreadnought*.

The USA granted the UK access to the technology needed to build *Dreadnought* but in return the UK had to accept strict conditions from Rickover that ensured American capitalism would profit from the construction. As an essential part of the deal, Rickover insisted that 'the Royal Navy should award its development work to a private company, and that in no way should the Navy rely on a Government Department to run the programme'.[11]

Article 13 of the 1958 Agreement specifically allowed the American Westinghouse Electric Corporation to sell the UK government a complete nuclear submarine propulsion plant, as well as the information required for the design, manufacture and operation of the reactor. In the end Rolls-Royce became the primary British agent for the manufacture of *Dreadnought*'s engine, with Westinghouse the U.S. agent. Vickers-Armstrongs was the shipbuilder. The construction of the first British nuclear submarine was therefore a joint business arrangement between Rolls-Royce and Westinghouse, with General Dynamics as the subcontractor. Five years later Britain's first SSBN, HMS *Resolution*, was launched, carrying Polaris nuclear missiles.

The post-war Soviet Union was keenly aware of the new challenge. Stalin, born in the nineteenth century, had favoured conventional battle fleets as the best expression of the USSR's superpower status. That view died with him. The new General Secretary of the Soviet Communist Party, Nikita Khrushchev, prioritized civilian infrastructure and industry over massive battleships. He also had new ideas about naval power. In 1956 he told an audience at the Royal Naval College, Greenwich, 'Today the submarine has come to the forefront as the chief naval weapon.'

In 1957 the USSR launched its first nuclear-powered attack submarine, the *K-3 Leninsky Komsomol*. The transformation of the Soviet submarine fleet from dilapidated diesel-electric vessels to a fleet of formidable SSNs and SSBNs was the work of Rickover's great antagonist, Admiral Sergey Gorshkov, Commander-in-Chief of the Soviet Navy, who had been appointed by Khrushchev in 1956 to revolutionize a force that had not distinguished itself during the last war. From the mid-1950s to the mid-1980s Gorshkov and Rickover engaged in a vicarious battle across the world's oceans for submarine supremacy.

Yet there was never really any doubt as to which force was superior. America's nuclear submarine fleet came to symbolize its political and strategic hegemony over the post-war world. Rickover was so closely associated with that hegemony that in 2014 Steve Bannon, head of the influential alt-right blog Breitbart News and (for a while) Donald Trump's key political advisor, produced a TV documentary about him entitled *Rickover: The Birth of Nuclear Power*, which praised the application of nuclear technology in the U.S. Navy and the role of nuclear submarines in containing the USSR.

Rickover emerged from a specific political milieu, one that funded and encouraged his messianic empire-building. The 1950s saw the height of McCarthyism and Cold War paranoia. American anti-Communist propaganda films such as *The Woman on Pier 13* (dir. Robert Stevenson, 1949), *I Was a Communist for the FBI* (dir. Gordon Douglas, 1951) and *Invasion, U.S.A.* (dir. Alfred E. Green, 1952) dramatized how the home front was threatened by subversive forces that were more embedded in American life than anyone suspected.

Hell and High Water (1954), directed by Sam Fuller, showcased the foreign threat. It centred on an American submarine uncovering and foiling a Chinese plan to frame the USA for a nuclear attack on the People's Republic, thus initiating a war between China and America that the villains assume China would then win. The film was a huge box-office success and established a clear narrative framework, repeated often, of the American military thwarting the nefarious schemes of a (usually undifferentiated) Communist bloc.

By the 1970s, when the process of détente cast a temporary calming influence over international relations, there was less interest in this kind of hyper-patriotism. The negotiating and signing of the Strategic Arms Limitation Treaty 1 (SALT 1) in 1972, and SALT 2 in 1979, led to a brief period of de-escalation on both sides, accompanied by new efforts to establish economic, cultural and scientific ties of mutual benefit. The new political zeitgeist inevitably impacted the submarine genre. Even James Bond, in the film *The Spy Who Loved Me* (dir. Lewis Gilbert, 1977), worked (closely, of course) with the KGB's Major Anya Amasova to foil the plans of an eco-terrorist who planned to use captured British and Russian SSBNs to destroy the world and start again underwater.

Unlike 1960s thrillers such as *Ice Station Zebra*, which explicitly pitted a U.S. nuclear submarine against Soviet adversaries in the Arctic, 1970s submarine dramas tended to focus on natural or technological disasters, and the resilience of the crew in surviving them. In that vein came *Gray Lady Down* (dir. David Greene, 1975), an unwieldy fusion of the submarine genre with the 1970s disaster movie in which a container ship with faulty radar collides with the American SSN *Neptune*, which then sinks to rest precariously on a crumbling ocean shelf. Despite a rugged performance by Charlton Heston as the *Neptune*'s captain, *Gray Lady Down* lacks both atmosphere and technical credibility, as if the absence of a clear political agenda had sapped its vitality.

Détente did not last, and even at its height was a shaky edifice. Incidents such as that in January 1973, when a Soviet submarine was detected in the Clyde near Faslane naval base, continued to stoke distrust. When fly-bys from RAF Nimrods failed to dislodge the intruder, the British SSN *Conqueror* received orders from the Ministry of Defence to 'sail forthwith and sweep the Russian from our waters'. It did so by luring the Soviet submarine out into the Atlantic and then diving deep to allow it to pass overhead.

There were similar incidents when American submarines entered Soviet territorial waters for covert surveillance, the most flagrant being routine U.S. tapping throughout the 1970s of a phone cable between Vladivostok and Petropavlovsk in the Sea of Okhotsk used by the Soviet Navy. An American SSN was required to secretly enter Soviet waters once every few months to retrieve the data recorded on the tap, occasionally coming close to detection.[12]

The 'phony war' of the 1970s soon morphed into the more openly confrontational politics of the 1980s. This did not always manifest as direct engagement between the USA and the Soviet Union. The re-emergence of the submarine onto the global political stage, and thereby into a new popular consciousness and fiction, was aided considerably by the most unexpected military conflict of the post-war years.

On 2 April 1982 Argentine military forces invaded and occupied the Falklands/Malvinas Islands, a British dependent territory 500 kilometres (310 mi.) off the coast of Argentina over which it had long claimed sovereignty. In response the UK sent a naval taskforce to reclaim the islands. The first vessel to set out, from Faslane naval base on 4 April, was British SSN HMS *Conqueror.* Just before departure the *Conqueror* took on board nine members of the Special Boat Squadron (SBS), whose mission was not revealed to the crew.[13] Four other British SSNs – *Spartan, Splendid, Courageous* and *Valiant* – set off soon after. With the *Conqueror* stopping to transfer its SBS commandos to a surface vessel off the island of South Georgia, the *Spartan* was the first submarine to reach the Falklands, where it began sending back intelligence information to British Naval Command in its bunker in Northwood, North London.

At the same time, the UN Security Council passed UN Resolution 502, which condemned the invasion. While it called for the UK and Argentina to work for a negotiated settlement, it agreed that the UK could invoke Article 51 of the UN Charter allowing the right of self-defence against armed attack. On 30 April the UK declared a 320-kilometre (200 nautical miles) 'Total Exclusion Zone' around the Falklands and stated that all ships of foreign nations should stay out or risk being fired upon. The declaration clarified that this was 'without prejudice to the right of the United Kingdom to take whatever additional measures may be needed in exercise of its right of self-defence, under Article 51 of the United Nations Charter'.

On 1 May *Conqueror* sighted the Argentine cruiser *General Belgrano* sailing southwest of the Falklands, just outside the TEZ, and radioed Northwood for orders. At this point there was disagreement between the Task Force Commander, Rear Admiral Sandy Woodward, who wished to fire upon the *Belgrano* immediately, and the Chief of the Defence Staff, Lord Lewin, who insisted that no action be taken without authorization from the War Cabinet. Notwithstanding that the *Belgrano* was outside the TEZ, Northwood asked the War Cabinet, presided over by Prime Minister Margaret Thatcher, for authority to sink the Argentine cruiser. After discussion, Thatcher gave authority to do so.

Just before 1600 hours on 2 May *Conqueror* launched three Mk 8 torpedoes at the *Belgrano*, the only combat torpedo shots ever fired by a nuclear submarine. The cruiser was hit twice, and within minutes it started to sink. Of a crew of 1,100 personnel, 323 were killed. After the attack all Argentine naval forces returned to their bases and played no further role in the conflict, which was conducted by land and air.

The headline of the tabloid *The Sun* the next day – 'Gotcha' – carved a dividing line across the home front that the populist right-wing press sustained ferociously.[14] One either enthusiastically supported the war up to and including the sinking of the *Belgrano*, and was therefore a right-minded patriot, or one did not and was therefore a closet traitor, what Thatcher would later describe as 'the enemy within'.

The emotional fallout from the war, and from the sinking of the *Belgrano* in particular, was made even more acute when the *Conqueror* returned to Faslane flying a Jolly Roger flag adorned with torpedoes. Although this was a long tradition for Royal Navy submarines going back to the First World War, some felt it tasteless in the circumstances. Later, replying to criticism of the sinking of the *Belgrano* while it was outside the TEZ, the *Conqueror*'s captain, Commander Christopher Wreford-Brown, was insouciant: 'The Royal Navy spent thirteen years preparing me for such an occasion. It would have been regarded as extremely dreary if I had fouled it up.'

The sinking of the *Belgrano* and the triumphalism that accompanied it elicited a powerful reaction from the Left exemplified by Paul Foot's *New Statesman* article of May 1983, 'Torpedoing the Peace', which asked:

> Did Mrs Thatcher order the sinking of the aged Argentine
> cruiser *General Belgrano*, on Sunday 2 May 1982, in order
> to scupper a peace settlement which had been hammered
> out between Lima, Peru, and Washington over the previous

The SSN HMS
Conqueror returns
to Faslane base flying
the Jolly Roger flag
of crossed torpedoes
and skull after
sinking Argentine
battleship *General
Belgrano* in the
Falklands, July 1982.

weekend and which was on the point of being signed? For
several months, Tam Dalyell, the Labour MP for West Lothian,
has been making this astonishing charge against the Prime
Minister. His view is that she deliberately gave the order
to sink the cruiser at a time when an honourable peace settlement was almost secured – one which could have prevented
the subsequent bloodshed of the Falklands campaign.

Foot's article encapsulated what became the Left's consensus view
of the sinking of the *Belgrano* – that Thatcher took a personal decision,
against the rules of engagement set up by the TEZ, to derail a potential
peace settlement that was near to completion. Sadly for that theory the
Peruvian ceasefire plan, prepared with U.S. assistance, was not 'on the

point of being signed' on 2 May, although the British government was aware of its existence and that it might constitute the basis of a settlement. It was also aware, through access to Argentine signals traffic, that the *Belgrano* was heading away from the TEZ and returning to its home base. There was no immediate need to sink it, but Thatcher did not override her naval commanders or impose an action on them that they did not first suggest.[15]

The British left, traumatized by the speed with which the political zeitgeist had lurched rightwards with a sudden explosion of war fever, produced an equally feverish response. The best example of this counter-hysteria is Steven Berkoff's play *Sink the Belgrano!* (1986), a satire in mock-Shakespearean verse that portrays a demented 'Maggot Scratcher', advised by her lieutenants Pimp and Nit, cynically sabotaging peace by a bloodthirsty decision to sink the *Belgrano*, a decision she takes alone and which is relayed to 'Command', the *Conqueror's* captain, to carry out.

Unfortunately, despite its technical virtuosity and flashes of linguistic wit, *Sink the Belgrano!*'s attack on Maggot Scratcher is so virulent that it backfires, failing to convince that the sinking of the *Belgrano* was, as Berkoff asserted, a 'calculated piece of sabotage'.[16] Nor does all of Berkoff's Shakespearean parody translate well to its subject-matter:

> TOMMY   Alright, we've heard the news, let's get stuck in,
>   And sail our deadly turd-shaped tube
>   That will unleash pure havoc when
>   Upon the surface of the deep we spy
>   Some vessel filled with Argentines.

Berkoff had a keen sense of his audience. Britain in the 1980s experienced a surge of anti-nuclear protests such as the Women's Peace Camp at Greenham Common and a similar camp, still running today, at Faslane in Scotland, where the UK's main base for nuclear submarines is situated (HMNB Clyde). The Faslane protest emerged from an Advisory Opinion of the International Court of Justice, which ruled that 'The threat or use of nuclear weapons would generally be contrary to the rules of international law applicable in armed conflict.'

On this basis of this Opinion from the ICJ, the anti-nuclear activist group Ploughshares has argued that since the British government was (and is) engaged in upgrading its Trident missile programme, whose only reason for existence is its threatened use, it is in violation of the Nuclear Non-Proliferation Treaty of 1968 to which it is a signatory. The same therefore applies to the U.S. government, whose growing fleet of Nuclear Ballistic Submarines (SSBNs, or 'boomers') is the ultimate guarantor of mutually assured destruction in the event of nuclear war.

What has been called 'the Second Cold War' – that is, that of the late 1970s and the '80s – was in many ways more dangerous than the first. In 1960 the rival arsenals of the USA and USSR had a total of 6,500 nuclear weapons. By 1979 this had risen to 14,200. In the early 1980s, following the deployment of SS20 nuclear missiles across the Soviet Bloc, the arrival of American Pershing missiles in western Europe, and Britain's replacement of Polaris with Trident, Cold War tensions reached a peak not seen since the 1950s.

The most significant cultural political by-product of this was the resurgence of the Campaign for Nuclear Disarmament (CND) and a wave of impassioned agit-prop around the issue of nuclear escalation, including the devastating British film *Threads* (1984) about the aftermath of a nuclear attack on Sheffield, Raymond Briggs's powerful graphic novel *When the Wind Blows* (1982) and popular songs such as Kate Bush's 'Breathing' (1980), Frankie Goes to Hollywood's 'Two Tribes' (1984) and Sting's 'Russians' (1985). On 12 June 1982, in the largest political demonstration in American history, a million people demonstrated in New York's Central Park against nuclear weapons and for an end to the new arms race.

The political response to this activity came not just from the re-elections of Thatcher and Reagan, but in blockbuster films such as

Rambo (1985) and *Top Gun* (1986) and in the submarine-themed techno-thriller, an artistically negligible yet culturally influential genre that emerged and took off in the 1980s and '90s. The genre includes a plethora of work in novel and film, but one product has come to stand for them all.

Tom Clancy's 1984 best-seller *The Hunt for Red October*, and its 1990 film adaptation directed by John McTiernan, require critical examination as the foundation stone and template of a modern sub-genre, in the same manner as the late nineteenth-century SF novels of H. G. Wells or J.R.R. Tolkien's *The Lord of the Rings*. President Reagan's praise of *The Hunt for Red October* as 'unputdownable' and 'the perfect yarn' not only boosted its sales but ensured Clancy dominated the military techno-thriller for the next two decades.

The story of the attempted defection to America of the Soviet Union's senior submarine captain Marko Ramius and his officers, along with the prototype SSBN *Red October* with its new 'silent propulsion' drive, *Red October* introduced Clancy's main protagonist, CIA analyst Jack Ryan, and founded a multimedia franchise. The first work of fiction published by the American Naval Institute Press, with whom Clancy had a close relationship (having written articles for its magazine *Proceedings of the U.S. Naval Institute*), *The Hunt for Red October* is literally political propaganda. Although his later work did not feature a nuclear submarine as a central component, novels such as *Red Storm Rising* (1986) and *The Sum of All Fears* (1991) included significant roles for American SSNs and stressed their importance to U.S. national security.

Clancy's early novels, in particular *Red October* and *Clear and Present Danger* (1989), successfully fuse loving descriptions of military hardware with rapid plots on the edge of credibility. His later books, in which Ryan becomes national security advisor and then U.S. president, are bloated and unreadable. But his romantic pro-Americanism gained him a vast and loyal 'Red State' readership, unconcerned that the politics he and Ryan espoused were essentially lawless, a glamorized and uncritical endorsement of international state terrorism as long as it was practised by the United States.

Clancy entirely lacks the artistry of popular novelists such as Ian Fleming or Stephen King. He cannot turn a phrase or coin a metaphor. His dialogue is often excruciating. His heroes have no interior life beyond a macho sentimentality and bonhomie. Aside from specialist knowledge required for work, and no matter their seniority in the intelligence or military services, they swear jocularly at each other and discuss 'the game' like Joe Six Pack. And yet, while he seldom achieves any lasting affect, his literary significance is considerable.

Before Clancy the nearest most thriller writers got to forensic technical detail were the descriptions of espionage tradecraft and small-scale ordnance found in writers like Frederick Forsyth or Len Deighton. Clancy shot far beyond that, detailing the specifications and capacities of hard and soft weapons systems, their computing and IT powers, their payloads and methods of delivery. Whether describing submarine navigation systems, aircraft missile guidance, CIA surveillance devices or basic military hardware such as tanks and Humvees, he indisputably knew his kit.

Clancy's rise to literary super-stardom was directly linked to Ronald Reagan. The dedication to Clancy's *Executive Orders* (1996) reads 'To President Ronald W. Reagan, the man who won the war.' Like Reagan, Clancy was massively popular with the U.S. armed forces, who indulged him with visits to top-secret bases and tours of nuclear submarines. When, in 1985, he visited the SSN *Hyman G. Rickover*, Clancy claimed to have found 25 copies of *The Hunt for Red October* on board. Art and life are seldom so entwined.

One reason for the success of the film of *Red October* was that it dispensed with Clancy's atrocious dialogue and mom-and-apple-pie Republicanism. It also benefited from energetic direction from John McTiernan, director of *Die Hard* (1988), and a commanding performance from Sean Connery as Ramius, whose motivation for defection was changed from anger at the preventable death of his wife through

Soviet incompetence to disgust at the *Red October*'s implied use as firststrike weapon. McTiernan also establishes a visual aesthetic for the
modern SSN that, although situated in the 1980s, transcends its period.
While the interiors of U.S. SSN *Dallas* are warmly lit, the *Red October*
is a miniature Death Star in gleaming red and black.

   Clancy's obsession with submarines was such that he wrote both
a non-fiction account of life on a U.S. nuclear submarine, *Submarine:
A Guided Tour Inside a Nuclear Warship* (1993), and a role-playing

Los Angeles-class
fast attack
submarine USS
Alexandria covered
in snow, Groton,
Connecticut, 2008.

multi-scenario book, *SSN* (1996). He also produced a video simulation game, *Red Storm Rising* (1988) – played initially on Commodore 64 and created by Sid Meier, designer of *Civilization* – in which the player assumes the character of the captain of an American SSN in the North Sea, with the mission of destroying Soviet submarines attempting to break through the GUIK Gap.

In contrast to the sub-textual politics of his novels, Clancy's non-fiction makes explicit that he is providing overt state propaganda to a mass audience. After examining every sub-system, element and section of the U.S. nuclear submarine USS *Miami*, Clancy considers its crew, and concludes,

> America can take pride in the sacrifices of these men and their loved ones over the last forty-five years of SSN operations. Pride for a job well done. Pride in what they are. And pride in what they will do in the future.[17]

After the demise of the Soviet Union in 1991 the main challenge facing the U.S. Department of Defense was how to justify continuation of its enormous military expenditure, not least the R&D and new product development underpinning much of the American economy. At no point did it reduce its annual budget requests to Congress. It simply replaced Soviet Communism with international terrorism, Islamic fundamentalism and rising superpowers such as China and Iran as threats to America that could only be met by a 'Full Spectrum Dominance' capability, that is, total control of air, land and sea in all important strategic regions.

A necessary and key component of Full Spectrum Dominance was a new generation of nuclear submarines. These were all the more essential to the USA, as the Soviet Union, in the last decade of its existence, unveiled a new and impressive generation of SSNs and SSBNs – the Akula-class attack submarines and the largest SSBNs ever constructed, the Typhoon class (Clancy's *Red October* is a Typhoon). The Typhoons could accommodate 160 crew in comfort and had the ability – if needed, in or after a world war – to sit for months under pack ice, surface and launch ICBMs with a range of 8,000 kilometres (5,000 mi.). They were game changers.

The Akula-class SSNs and Typhoon-class SSBNs were inherited by the post-Soviet Russian Navy. Although only six Typhoons were ever built (and were extremely expensive to maintain) their very existence was one reason why since 1991 the U.S. Navy has built up the largest fleet of SSBNs in the world.

After the fall of the Soviet Union the Russian Navy shrank to a quarter of the size of the USSR's at its height, its submarine force collapsing from almost four hundred vessels in 1985 to just 63 in 2008. But then it began to rebuild. In recent years the rapid expansion of the Russian and Chinese submarine fleets has re-emphasized to U.S. military planners the need to maintain and expand their own fleet. In 2018 a senior RAND Corporation defence researcher confirmed: 'There is no greater priority for the US Navy than SSBN recapitalization.'[18]

The creation of a post-Soviet new world order maintained by the American military required a fresh popular narrative on and about the operations of U.S. armed forces. The success of *The Hunt for Red October* demonstrated that those with the skill to formulate it would reap massive financial rewards. Clancy's major successor in this regard was the British novelist Patrick Robinson, who between 1997 and 2008 produced ten best-selling techno-thrillers that either centred on or had important roles for American SSNs and SSBNs.

In *Kilo Class* (1998) Robinson's dubious 'hero' Admiral Arnold Morgan is the architect of a U.S. covert operation to sink a number of Kilo-class Russian submarines that Russia has sold to China and which are about to be delivered. The sale is not fictional. Since the fall of the Soviet Union a number of diesel-electric Kilo-class submarines – renowned for their 'potent power projection capabilities' and 'high survivability and flexible weapons systems' – have been sold by Russia to China, India, Algeria, Romania and Iran.[19]

Although there was, and is, nothing secret or illegal about this purchase, in *Kilo Class* Robinson has the U.S. government decide it must prevent any of the submarines being delivered, because – so the thinking is explained – once China takes possession it would have the capacity to blockade and invade Taiwan, over which it has claimed sovereignty since 1949.

Morgan tells the Chief of Naval Operations that with the submarines shortly about to depart for China, 'I have suggested to the President that we may have to arrange for them not to arrive home. NOT EVER. Devious Chinese pricks.'[20] Morgan therefore orders an SSN commanded by the rugged 'Boomer' Dunning to covertly track, ambush and sink the first two submarines while they are en route to China. The operation succeeds, first by sinking the two submarines off the Faroe Islands, then by deploying undercover Navy SEALs *within* Russia to sabotage a third, and then by ambushing another in exceptionally dangerous

Russian Akula-class nuclear-powered attack submarine (SSN) offshore in Ukraine, June 2006.

circumstances off Taiwan. None of Robinson's characters exhibit con-
cern that by any standard of international law the operation is an act
of terrorism resulting in the deaths of hundreds of innocent people.

Robinson's main competitor as Clancy's successor, Michael
DiMercurio, is a more engaging writer. Unlike Robinson and Clancy,
DiMercurio served on American nuclear submarines as a communications officer and a chief propulsion officer and upon leaving the navy
turned to writing semi-futuristic techno-thrillers set on board SSNs.
As an ex-submariner, he is contemptuous of Clancy, stating, 'His *Hunt
for Red October* was a gigantic disappointment. It was nothing like
reality. It lacked the taste and feel of a nuclear submarine, the tension,
the drama, the terror of living at the edge of death. The book had
no soul.'[21]

Although DiMercurio's descriptions of SSN operational procedures
are more granular than Clancy's and his protagonist, Captain Michael
Pacino, is more interesting than Jack Ryan, his early novels do not
advance beyond the clichés of *The Hunt for Red October*. Their villains
are rogue Russian communists seeking to restore Soviet power (*Voyage
of the Devilfish*, 1992), and extremist Chinese communists engaged in
an unlikely Chinese civil war (*Attack of the Seawolf*, 1994), both of
whom gain control over lethal SSBNs and plan to use them against
the USA.

In his third novel, *Phoenix Sub Zero* (1994), the threat to America
comes from 'a thirty nation coalition called the United Islamic Front
of God, spanning all of North Africa, most of the Arabian peninsula,
and half of Asia', which has just begun the invasion of India.[22] In response
the USA and the nations of western Europe form the 'Western Coalition',
now at war with the Islamic Front. The UIFG, led by charismatic dicta-
tor General Mohammed al-Sihoud, also known as the 'Sword of Islam',
uses its oil riches to buy and augment a 'super-submarine' called the
Hegira. When a drone strike fails to assassinate Sihoud, he seeks refuge
on the *Hegira*, which escapes from the Mediterranean into the Atlantic
with the intention of firing its nuclear missiles at Washington, DC.

In DiMercurio's latter novels the USA, having defeated the Islamic Front, intervenes directly in the Chinese civil war to aid White China against Red China. Running out of challenges for by-then Admiral Pacino and his Unified Submarine Command to defeat, DiMercurio switched to a new series about U.S. submarine commander Peter Vornado, set in the present day. But after two Vornado adventures (*Emergency Deep*, 2004, and *Vertical Dive*, 2005) he appeared to lose inspiration and ceased writing.

His immediate successor, Joe Buff, keeps things fresh by making the threat to world peace an improbable alliance of white supremacist super-states. Writing in 2000 of the near-future of 2011, Buff has Boer-led reactionaries seize control of South Africa and restore Apartheid. After the UN impose a trade embargo, the South African government forms a military alliance with a new far-right regime in Germany which comes to power following the collapse of the EU. This is the basis of Buff's Jeffrey Fuller series, a six-novel saga running from *Deep Sound Channel* (2000) to *Seas of Crisis* (2006).

In the first novel the Boer-Berlin Axis uses small, tactical nuclear weapons to destroy Warsaw and Tripoli, whereupon most European nations surrender and are overrun by the new fascist alliance. Opposing the Axis stands the Allies, a coalition of forces led by the USA with support from the UK, Australia, Canada, Mexico, Brazil, Israel, Chile and Cuba. Buff's protagonist commands the USA's most advanced SSN and plays a key role in a twenty-first-century high-tech version of the Battle of the Atlantic in which the Axis attack Allied shipping using 'ceramic-composite-hulled' attack submarines supplied to them by Russia.

The modern prince of the submarine techno-thriller, Rick Campbell, served on American SSNs and SSBNs, being promoted to the position of XO. Beginning with *The Trident Deception* (2014), Campbell has utilized every trope of the genre in a series of fast-paced but increasingly preposterous thrillers which rely on the USA's main competitors for superpower status, Russia and China, risking a Third World War by taking extreme actions such as the invasion of the Baltic States and Taiwan. Campbell's *Ice Station Nautilus* (2016) crams as much submarine iconography as possible into one short title, the icing on the cake of a story of two SSBNs, one American and one Russian, that collide in the Arctic and require rescue by their nations' special commandoes – SEALs and *Spetsnaz* – with predictable results.

Campbell exemplifies the problem of the modern submarine-themed techno-thriller. Notwithstanding the occasional plot excursion and jolt of excitement, its primary characteristic is its homogeneity and predictability. Unlike the best of the detective and SF genres it has little stylistic flair or intellectual originality. Its narratives are driven by traditional masculinity and military technology. Its prose is invariably flat and prosaic. The sea, as a living ecology, is seldom mentioned at all, except as a set of grid coordinates the submarine must traverse in order to fire missiles or offload a SEAL team.

Despite its infatuation with advanced technology, the genre is deeply conservative. Its heroes are straight white military men or CIA operatives, bourgeois in every sense. 'The movie's set in California – people out there are a little crazy,' says Jack Ryan, speaking for them all.[23] They affect to be apolitical but have a religious faith in the values of venture capitalism. The country they uncritically serve is a Republican fantasy, a rich, free, technologically advanced yet non-aggressive super-power beset by fanatics on all sides. This concoction attracts a loyal readership of millions, mainly in the USA, but it remains a subculture in every sense of the word, finding its core audience in the white male demographic that propelled Donald Trump to the presidency.

While the submarine novel continues to trot out reliable clichés to a reliable audience, there are signs that film and TV may be rejecting them. BBC's *Vigil*, while engaging in the standard tropes of the genre such as a rapidly flooding compartment and a nerve-shredding plunge to crush depth, spent as much time on land, spicing its plot with the politics of Trident renewal, Faslane peace camps and security service surveillance of anti-nuclear activist groups. Although *Vigil* ultimately reinforces the politics of the nuclear deterrent (a Russian ploy to knock out the UK's one operational SSBN is implicitly accepted as leaving the UK 'defenceless'), it is not unsympathetic in its portrayal of the anti-Trident camp and the doomed couple, peace activist Jade and sonar operator Burke, who attempt to reveal how dysfunctional HMS *Vigil* has become.

The doctrine of Full Spectrum Dominance developed in the 1990s was itself dysfunctional. It rested on a fundamental overestimation of America's economic and military resources, since undermined by failed interventions in Iraq and Afghanistan and robust push backs from Russia and China. By 2018 Russia had a total of thirty SSNs and SSBNs combined, plus fifteen Kilo-class submarines, and had successfully flexed its military muscles in Ukraine and Syria. China is now rushing to catch up, developing new robotic and AI-enabled submarines to add to the SSNs shortly to roll out of its 'submarine factory' at Huludao on the Yellow Sea, an assembly hall so large that it can construct four SSNs simultaneously.[24]

Escalation continues elsewhere, from the Middle East, where Israel and Iran are upgrading their submarine fleets, to Asia. In July 2018 the Indian Navy announced plans to build six new nuclear submarines in response to China's expansion into the Indian Ocean, including the presence of Chinese warships in the strategically important port of Gwadar in Pakistan.[25]

In July 2016 the British House of Commons voted by a large majority to proceed with building a new fleet of four Dreadnought-class submarines to replace the UK's current Vanguard-class SSBNs, to be operational by 2028. Like the Vanguard fleet, these will carry Trident IID-5 ballistic missiles able to deliver thermonuclear warheads from Multiple Independently Targetable Re-entry Vehicles (MIRVs). The estimated cost of constructing the new SSBNs is £31 billion, but additional costs – in contingency funds, replacement warheads, infrastructure capital costs, in-service costs and conventional military forces to support Trident – push that total to an estimated £205 billion.[26]

In March 2021 Boris Johnson's Conservative government announced an increase in the total number of the UK's stockpiled Trident nuclear warheads for the first time since the height of the Cold War, reversing the UK government's previous commitment to reduce its total stockpile to 180 by the mid-2020s with a commitment to increase it to 260. At the same time the Ministry of Defence (MOD) announced that Russian submarines had 'taken a deep interest' in the UK's critical undersea communications cables. Faced with this apparent threat, the MOD is to build a new 'Multi Role Ocean Surveillance Ship' fitted with advanced sensors and remotely operated undersea drones to detect and deter Russian submarines. The new ship is due to come into service in 2024.

The UK is not the only country investing vast and arguably unnecessary sums in a new generation of submarines and their warheads. In 2016 Australia signed a $90 billion contract with France for the delivery of twelve new Attack-class diesel-electric submarines, to become operational by 2030. An Australian government defence white paper predicted that by 2035 half of the world's submarine fleet will be operating in the Indo-Pacific region.[27] The world is now experiencing a build-up of submarine fleets not seen since the decade before the First World War. As of 2018, the USA still has the largest submarine force – fourteen SSBNs and fifty SSNs set against Russia's twelve and eighteen, and China's five of each. The USA has begun construction of its first Columbia-class SSBN to replace the older Ohio class, aiming to have twelve new 'boomers' by 2040. By 2025 Russia will have constructed four more Borei-II submarines, the replacement for the mighty Typhoons, able to travel at 30 knots, 10 knots faster than America's new Columbia-class SBNs.[28] In October 2016 two Akula-class SSNs were detected in the Irish Sea and one Kilo-class in the English Channel, all en route to support Russian military operations in Syria. In February 2022 Russian submarines entered the Black Sea to support Russia's invasion of Ukraine.

This is not a stable balance of power. In September 2021 Australia suddenly pulled out of its deal with France to deliver a fleet of diesel-electric submarines for the Australian Navy, opting instead for a new generation of nuclear-powered submarines provided by the USA and the UK. The fallout was immediate. Diplomatic relations between France and Australia were severely strained, as France had been given no warning that a vital economic contract painstakingly negotiated had simply been abandoned. China, the intended target of the new 'security alliance' of Australia, the USA and the UK, reacted with predictable hostility, bringing up once again the subject of its claim to Taiwan, and the probability of renewed conflict in the Indo-Pacific region. Nuclear submarines will be at the forefront of that conflict.

All the elements are now in place, including military escalation, populist nationalism and a naive belief – fuelled in part by sleek techno-thrillers that present the nuclear submarine as a dazzling display of hot-rod technological prowess and disguising the genocidal nature of its weaponry – that a nuclear war is winnable and containable. If that belief is widely accepted, then hypothetical and vicarious wars will quickly mutate into the war-gaming strategies of contending superpowers. At that point Armageddon is only one garbled order away.

3

THE SUBMARINE
AND CATASTROPHE

The last American ship sunk in the Second World War was torpedoed by Japanese submarine *I-58* on 30 July 1945. The heavy cruiser USS *Indianapolis* was returning to Pearl Harbor from the island of Tinian in the Pacific, where it had delivered crucial components of 'Little Boy', the atomic bomb to be dropped on Hiroshima. The *Indianapolis* was hit by two torpedoes and sank quickly, leaving approximately nine hundred survivors out of a crew of 1,195. Because of the classified nature of its mission, it had been proceeding under radio silence and so for several days no one was aware it had been sunk. Many of the survivors died of exposure, dehydration and, most horrifically, mass shark attacks. By 2 August only 316 of the original survivors were still alive to be picked up by rescue planes and patrol boats. It remains the U.S. Navy's worst loss of life from a single ship at sea in its history.

The *Indianapolis* has entered contemporary culture on several levels and for several reasons – the bomb parts it delivered ensured that the first atomic bomb used in wartime was ready and able to instantly erase 60,000 lives when dropped on Hiroshima on 6 August; the awful, quasi-mythical fate of its crew, which smacks of divine retribution for their role in an unspeakable crime; and the dramatic retelling of that story by the grizzled shark hunter Quint (Robert Shaw) in one of the most successful films of all time, Steven Spielberg's *Jaws* (1975). Rarely, though, is its nemesis given as much attention.

By 1960 the submarine was no longer a smaller predator tracking bigger killers. It *was* the bigger killer, the apex predator, the bringer of mass destruction and nuclear fire. SSBNs changed the geo-strategic game completely and forever. The US's SSBNs carried sixteen Polaris A1 Missiles with a range of 1,900 kilometres (1,200 mi.), which were intended to be fired out of Earth's atmosphere before re-entering to home in on their targets. In terms of combined destructive power, the missile payload of one SSBN exceeded the total of all the bombs dropped in the Second World War.

Any consideration of the cultural meaning of the submarine must therefore confront the underlying raison d'être of the modern SSBN. This is to deter enemies from attacking the host nation through the credible threat of mass murder and, should the political situation demand it, to commit that mass murder. The SSN has a formidable strike capability and its missiles can lay waste to large areas but an SSBN is a radically different machine. It is an 'Omega' weapon. Any one could destroy human civilization on its own.[1]

That the SSBN is a weapon that cannot be used does not mean that it will not be used. The Bulletin of Atomic Scientists (founded in 1945 by remorseful Manhattan Project scientists to keep the public better informed about atomic power) maintains the famous 'Doomsday Clock', whereby it calculates how close the human race is to the symbolic 'midnight' of total annihilation. In January 2019 the Bulletin's Science and Security Board set the Doomsday Clock at two minutes to midnight.

The Board's statement noted:

> Humanity now faces two simultaneous existential threats, either of which would be cause for extreme concern and immediate attention. These major threats – nuclear weapons and climate change – were exacerbated this past year by the increased use of information warfare to undermine democracy around the world . . . The 'new abnormal' that we describe, and that the

world now inhabits, is unsustainable and extremely dangerous. The world security situation can be improved, if leaders
seek change and citizens demand it. It is 2 minutes to midnight,
but there is no reason the Doomsday Clock cannot move away
from catastrophe.[2]

Presenting the 'adventures' of an SSN or SSBN without reference to
this reality is akin to assessing the history of British imperialism solely
through the lens of romantic narratives such as *Zulu* or *The Four
Feathers*. The political effect of such romanticism is to obscure what a
nuclear submarine is and what it can do: destroy humanity; commit a
blanket massacre of civilian men, women and children through the
press of a button.

The innate dangers, the lethal undercurrent, of submarine life are
at the heart of the genre's finest products. John Ford's *Men Without
Women* (1930) is the outstanding submarine film of the interwar period,
despite subsequent mutilation of its film stock, which renders it difficult to fully assess. It was originally filmed with sound, but no complete
version now exists, as the film was re-edited with the dialogue scenes
replaced by screen captions in the style of silent cinema. The only
remaining print of Ford's masterpiece is a disjointed fusion of sound
and screen dialogue titles, with some scenes switching several times
between the two.

Its title taken from Hemingway's collection of short stories published in 1927, *Men Without Women* is set in the South China Sea and
takes place in the present time (that is, the time of its making). It intro-
duces what would become one of the main tropes of the submarine
genre, that of the sunken submarine with the clock ticking down to
rescue or death. For its time it is astonishingly visceral, an escalating
series of physical and emotional hammer blows as water rises inside the
sub, and electrical conduits short-circuit.

The crew of the sunken *s-13* quickly fall apart. Their captain already
dead, they fight over the one remaining oxygen tank. One breaks down

under stress and tries to blow up the submarine with a grenade. The chief engineer is the only one to maintain professional discipline. Only at the close, as the men use an unblocked torpedo tube to exit the submarine one by one to the waiting rescuers above, does a vestige of dignity prevail. As often within the genre, the underlying psychological stresses of submarine life arise as an offshoot of a more conventional plotline such as a unique wartime mission or a terrible accident.

Like *Men Without Women*, the British film *Morning Departure* (1950; released in the U.S. under the title *Operation Disaster*) takes the latter route. Focusing on a submarine accident in which most of the crew are killed, its opening titles are preceded by a statement about the decision to release the film in the light of the loss of the British submarine HMS *Truculent*, which in January 1950 collided with a Swedish oil tanker in the foggy Thames Estuary. Although the *Truculent* sank quickly, most of its crew survived the collision, but while a few were picked up in a lifeboat the remainder died of freezing cold on the mud islands of the estuary. The incident took place between the filming of *Morning Departure* and its release. After considering delaying release the producers went ahead, stressing in the preface that the film was offered as 'a tribute to the officers and men of HM Submarines'.

Morning Departure was dogged by ill omens. It was released just after the loss at sea of the Royal Navy submarine HMS *Affray* in April 1951. *Affray* was on a brief training exercise in the English Channel when suddenly all contact with it was lost. A massive search was launched, which ended two months later when a search vessel made sonar contact with the submarine on the bottom of Hurd's Deep, an underwater valley in the English Channel used by the UK government to dump unwanted munitions and nuclear waste from the 1940s to the 1970s. The *Affray*'s hull appeared undamaged and there was no indication of what had caused it to sink. Its crew remain entombed within it to this day.

Based on a play by Kenneth Woolard, *Morning Departure* begins with the British submarine HMS *Trojan*, like the real-life *Affray*, departing Plymouth for a simple one-day training exercise offshore. But the *Trojan* strikes an unrecovered Second World War mine and sinks to the bottom of the English Channel, with most of its crew killed. Twelve remain alive in the front section, awaiting rescue as their air runs out. With limited air canisters, only eight survivors can exit via the outer hatches. After the first four get out, there is a card draw for the final four. The captain (John Mills) does not draw a card.

Nominated for Best Film at the 1951 BAFTA Awards, *Morning Departure* is a tense and affecting study of how barriers of rank and class dissolve under abnormal pressure. Its close, as the submarine's painfully slow rescue is called off because of a storm that threatens the salvage ship's safety, and the remaining crew (the captain, Richard Attenborough's troubled stoker and James Hayter's chipper cook) resign themselves to death, is restrained and moving.

Morning Departure occupies a unique position in submarine film chronology. It is not of or about the Second World War, but neither is it about the Cold War. It is not a thriller or a military adventure. It is not a fraught drama of emotional collapse: aside from Attenborough's one fit of hysteria, from which he quickly recovers, the survivors are professional throughout. It is a British submarine story par excellence, a tale of brave men facing an early death because of bad luck and bad weather.

In the late 1950s, as McCarthyism waned, cultural space opened up for examinations of where the Cold War might ultimately lead – nuclear war. Nevil Shute's novel *On the Beach* (1957) was an unflinching vision of the aftermath of such a war, in which most of the world has been destroyed except Australia and New Zealand. But survival is short-lived, as radiation clouds will shortly blanket the entire globe. Shute's novel focuses on a group of people in Melbourne, Australia, including the crew of the U.S. submarine *Scorpion*, as they await death, either by radiation poisoning or by government-supplied suicide pills.

'On the beach' was a Royal Navy term meaning 'retired from service'. The *Scorpion* is in every sense retired, as it has no enemy to fight or homeland to which it can return. Its one mission during the story, a trip to Seattle to investigate a mysterious radio signal, is futile, as the signal is found to be simply the result of a window sash randomly hitting a telegraph key. At the close all the characters face death in various ways, and the *Scorpion* is taken out to sea and scuttled.

There is little overt drama in *On the Beach* beyond the closing in of relentless mortality. It is a deeply affecting hymn to life's small pleasures and loves, and an indictment of humanity's stupidity in bringing them to a total and sudden end. Although films such as *The War Game* (1965) and *Threads* (1984) portrayed the horrendous physical impact of a nuclear attack on civilian infrastructure, Shute's novel located the sheer existential tragedy of nuclear war.

The film adaptation of *On the Beach* (1959) was equally gruelling. Aside from changing the submarine's name to *Sawfish* and developing the doomed romance between its captain (Gregory Peck) and a Melbourne socialite (Ava Gardner), Stanley Kramer's film was as saturated in tragic despair as its source material. It retained Shute's key narrative beats – the erosion of hope as the radiation clouds drift further south, the 'end times' partying, the failed submarine mission – and allowed not the slightest chink of light. At the close Peck forsakes his new love to do his duty by his crew, taking them back to an irradiated America to die, and Melbourne is left empty and lifeless after its remaining citizens take their pills.

Predicting nuclear apocalypse did not prevent its near-arrival. In October 1962 American spy satellites discovered Soviet nuclear missiles had been installed on Cuba, meaning they could reach targets in America much quicker. Although the USA had recently installed nuclear missiles in Turkey on the USSR's southern border, President John F. Kennedy was urged by his joint chiefs of staff to launch an immediate invasion of Cuba.[3] Fearing this would escalate to nuclear war, he instead imposed a naval blockade. Soviet ships would be stopped and searched before proceeding and no further weapons would be allowed to pass, while missiles already there would have to be dismantled and returned home.

With U.S. military forces at DEFCON 3 (**Def**ense **Con**dition 3), the highest they had ever been, U.S. submarines in the region were primed and ready to fire. In turn, the Soviet Navy sent some of its diesel-powered submarines to test American ships enforcing the blockade.[4] On 27 October the U.S. Navy destroyer *Cony* dropped a number of 'signalling' depth charges (smaller depth charges the size of hand grenades) on the Foxtrot-class Soviet attack submarine *B-59*, unaware that the submarine had orders that if it were attacked it was to fire its nuclear-tipped torpedoes.

The depth charges were only intended to flush out the submarine, not destroy it, yet the duration and intensity of a day's bombardment drove the *B-59*'s captain to the end of his tether. Since the *B-59* was too deep to receive radio signals, he assumed that war had commenced and decided to fire at the American destroyer. However, the command to launch required agreement from the First Officer, Vasili Arkhipov, who kept a cooler head and refused to do so.[5] Had the *B-59* fired its nuclear torpedoes and vaporized the *Cony*, nuclear war would certainly have followed.

On the same day the *B-59* nearly fired a nuclear torpedo, Kennedy and Khrushchev exchanged letters and began to de-escalate the situation. Despite its peaceful resolution, the trauma of the Cuban Missile Crisis left a lasting impact that shifted popular perception of the nuclear deterrent and its means of delivery. In the 1960s anti-Communist propaganda films began to mutate into anti-war films. One of the most notable, *The Bedford Incident* (dir. James B. Harris, 1965), spooled back to the final days before the nuclear apocalypse to demonstrate how it might arrive.

Drawing from the *B-59* incident, the film focuses on a tense stand-off between an American destroyer, USS *Bedford*, commanded by the psychotic Captain Finlander (Richard Widmark), and a Soviet submarine off the coast of Greenland. Observed by an increasingly appalled civilian journalist (Sidney Poitier), Finlander, passed over for promotion because of his vocal support for a nuclear attack on

Cuba during the Missile Crisis, plays cat and mouse with the submarine, driving his crew to exhaustion. In the end the apocalypse arrives by accident when a tired ensign mishears Finlander's instructions and launches a torpedo at the submarine, which fires back. The film ends in mutual nuclear annihilation and a searing image of the film stock burning on the screen.

Alistair MacLean's thriller *Ice Station Zebra* (1963) was published immediately after the Missile Crisis. Following the secret mission of the U.S. SSN *Dolphin* to extricate stranded scientists at the ice station of the title, the plot twists and turns as the real explanation for the mission is gradually revealed. After a Soviet spy satellite crashes near Zebra, the base scientists discover it contains secret film of all U.S. nuclear missile launch sites. The narrator, a British spy on board the *Dolphin* sent to retrieve the film before the Soviets, is forced to rely on the ingenuity of its crew when one of the submarine's torpedo tubes, sabotaged by an on-board Russian spy to read as shut when its exterior door is in fact open, is opened from the inside. With the torpedo room instantly flooded, the submarine plunges to near destruction.

MacLean's novel has more in common with the procedural realism of Len Deighton than the elitist glamour of Ian Fleming. It drew from several real-life submarine exploits such as the passage under the North Pole of USS *Nautilus* in 1955, and the visit by the nuclear submarine USS *Skate* to the American scientific base Ice Station Alpha in the Arctic in 1958. Deighton's own *Spy Story* (1974) repackaged some elements of *Ice Station Zebra*, notably the use of a nuclear submarine to retrieve British spies from the Arctic after a dangerous mission.

The film of *Ice Station Zebra* (1968), directed by John Sturges, took the core of the story but ramped it up to include Soviet fighter jets, paratroopers and a tense military stand-off at Zebra. A classic example of an old-school big-screen adventure, it retains undeniable charm as the quintessential Cold War submarine/espionage film, cemented by muscular performances from Rock Hudson and Patrick McGoohan as the stolid submarine captain and devious British agent.

Ice Station Zebra was unusual in conceding that the USSR possessed a technological resource that the West coveted, for aside from its space programme – presided over by the brilliant 'Chief Designer' Sergei Korolev, father of the Intercontinental Ballistic Missile – Soviet military technology was comparatively sub-par. In comparison to the U.S.'s Permit- and Sturgeon-class SSNs (the default designs of U.S. nuclear submarines from the late 1950s to the early 1970s) the USSR's first class of nuclear submarines, the November class, were unreliable and prone to accidents, some of which were major and life-threatening.[6]

One of the worst of these was an incident in July 1961 when the Soviet SSBN *K-19*, on its maiden voyage off the southern coast of Greenland, suffered a major leak in its reactor coolant system, threatening a meltdown and a thermonuclear explosion. With few options, the captain ordered the engineering crew to jury-rig a water-cooling system, which meant entering the reactor chamber and working in high

Crew members monitor equipment in the control room aboard the nuclear-powered attack submarine USS *Pargo* (SSN-650) while north of the Arctic Circle, April 1991.

radiation for extended periods. The effort was successful but led to the death through radiation exposure of the entire repair crew.

K-19: The Widowmaker (2002), a powerful and underrated film directed by Kathryn Bigelow, director of *The Hurt Locker* and the first woman to win an Academy Award for Best Director, retells this incident. A literate screenplay neatly establishes character, particularly that of the former captain and now XO Polenin (Liam Neeson), who sees himself as the father of the boat, and the steely new captain Vostrikov (Harrison Ford), who, although well aware of the strategic and political failings of his masters, is tasked with taking the *K-19* under Arctic ice to test-fire a new missile and cannot afford to be sympathetic to his crew if the mission is to be achieved.

A brief opening scene of a missile-launching test establishes that there are basic flaws in the *K-19*'s electronics components. Even before the accident the *K-19* had earned a reputation as a cursed boat because of the catalogue of deaths involved in its construction. In the film the submarine is already known as 'the Widowmaker' before it departs on its mission. In reality it had no nickname prior to the mission, although after its return it was informally referred to by Soviet submarine crews as 'Hiroshima'.

The film skilfully fills in this context. Just before departure the submarine's doctor chases after a lorry that has delivered the wrong medicine and is accidentally killed by another vehicle. The *K-19* is ordered to sea before all safety checks can be completed. The submarine's safety manual refers to a back-up system that has not been installed. Instead of the radiation suits required, the submarine has chemical suits, which offer no protection from radiation. Despite this the engineering crew fix the reactor, prevent a nuclear meltdown that would have consumed a nearby American destroyer, and possibly save the world.

The final scenes, as the burnt, blinded and vomiting repair crew repeatedly re-enter the irradiated chamber while slowly succumbing to fatal injuries, is genuinely affecting, a real and uncondescending ode to Soviet bravery. Towards the close the film suffers from a lack of nerve,

Liam Neeson in *k-19:
The Widowmaker*
(2002, dir. Kathryn
Bigelow).

adding an unnecessary and unhistorical mutiny against Vostrikov by
the cowardly *Zamyotin* (political officer) and an overly sentimental
ending, but it tells a tale worth telling with some integrity.

So, too, does *Hostile Waters* (1997), a BBC–HBO co-production
which drew on an incident in October 1986 in which the Soviet SSBN
K-219, engaged in a routine patrol in the North Atlantic, suffered a leak
in one of its missile tubes, causing a catastrophic explosion. The *K-219*
took on seawater and plummeted to a depth of nearly 3,000 metres
(1,000 ft), where it managed to stabilize itself. Only the bravery of a
junior seaman, who entered the reactor chamber to shut it down (and
died in doing so), prevented a nuclear explosion. After surfacing the
captain defied his orders to stay on the flooded and irradiated submarine and transferred his crew to a rescue trawler. The fatally damaged
K-219 then plunged 5,500 metres (18,000 ft) to the bottom of an
abyssal plain.

The film and the book upon which it is based claim that the leak
was caused by a collision with a U.S. submarine, which the USA and
Russia both deny. The history told in the book, co-written by retired
U.S. naval captain Peter Huchthausen and Russian Captain First Rank
Igor Kurdin (the *K-219*'s XO), was reconstructed from survivors' accounts,

ships' logs and investigation reports. Its thesis of a collision is credible but not essential. The core of the drama is the vulnerability of a nuclear submarine's reactor to accident, and the sacrifices required to contain it.

The vulnerability of a nuclear submarine was never more cruelly illustrated than in the fate of the Russian Oscar-class SSN *Kursk*, the subject of the harrowing French–Belgian film *Kursk* (2018). In August 2000, on a training exercise in the Barents Sea, a faulty torpedo exploded in one of the *Kursk's* launch tubes, destroying its forward two compartments. As per emergency procedures the submarine's nuclear reactor immediately shut down but a few minutes later rising temperatures in the remaining sections set off seven more torpedoes. The resultant explosion registered 4.2 on the Richter scale. Most of the 118-man crew were killed instantly but 23 survivors led by a junior lieutenant were trapped in a sealed aft compartment with rapidly diminishing oxygen.

The Russian Navy was criminally slow to mobilize, waiting 11 hours before declaring an emergency. Offers of help from Norway and Britain, who had ships with specialized rescue submersibles in the vicinity, were rejected for five days, by which time it was too late. It may always have been. But regardless of whether international assistance might have effected a rescue, the Russian authorities initially treated the crew's families with callous indifference. For a while the blowback damaged President Vladimir Putin himself, who was caught on camera being screamed at by distraught relatives. Thereafter, in direct response to his public humiliation, Putin imposed firmer control on the Russian media.

The film *Kursk* is a brutal wake-up call for a genre lost in romantic militarism, focusing as much on the struggle of the crews' families against a state whose main priority is to protect itself as on the grim drama unfolding at sea. It is a powerful and poignant memorial to the crew of the *Kursk*, a reminder that the strategic games played by nuclear submarines – in the works of Clancy, Robinson and Campbell, as well as in the Atlantic, the Baltic and the Indian Ocean – ride on the backs of working-class crews who work and live in cramped and dangerous conditions, and who face a terrible death if those games misfire.

The vicarious enjoyment the games provide is too lucrative a market not to exploit. In 2018 the videogame studio JuJubee SA released *Kursk*, a first-person 'action and survival game' available on PC, Mac, PlayStation 4 and Xbox One. In the game the player assumes the role of a spy on board the *Kursk*, whose role is 'to collect secret information about the revolutionary Shkval supercavitating torpedoes'. In a dim echo of the smooth reframing of pretexts required for the continued production of American SSNs and SSBNs after the fall of the Soviet Union, the makers of the game promise that players will 'Experience the history of the fateful voyage of *K-141* KURSK that ended at the bottom of the Barents Sea', and can do so over and over again.

American popular culture might occasionally concede that Soviet submariners could be brave and selfless as long as it is firmly established that their vessels, and by extension their society, are unworthy of them. By contrast, U.S. submarines might encounter jeopardy by accident or unforeseen disaster (such as in *Gray Lady Down*) but not through inherent flaws of leadership, ideology or technology. Yet evidence of problems in their own submarine fleet was well known. In April 1963 the American SSN *Thresher* sank suddenly off Portsmouth, New Hampshire, while conducting routine post-overhaul trials, with the loss of all its 129 crew. Although the shattered remains of the *Thresher* were found by deep-diving bathyspheres 2,560 metres (8,400 ft) below the surface, it was impossible to determine what had caused the disaster. At the time *Thresher* was considered the fastest and quietest submarine ever built, and its loss was a severe blow to the U.S. Navy. In response it instituted a radical new programme called the Submarine Safety Program (SUBSAFE).

SUBSAFE is a set of safety procedures designed to provide the maximum possible assurance that submarine hulls will stay watertight and that they can recover quickly from unanticipated flooding. It ensures that all submarine systems exposed to sea pressure or that assist

Memorial in honour of the 129 men lost aboard USS *Thresher* (SSN-593) on 10 April 1963, Arlington National Cemetery, Washington, DC.

flooding recovery are rigorously certified at every stage of construction and installation. Since the inception of the SUBSAFE programme the U.S. Navy has lost only one submarine, the non-SUBSAFE-certified SSN *Scorpion* in May 1968. The reason why the *Scorpion* sank has also never been confirmed.

Although the U.S Navy has not lost an entire SUBSAFE-certified submarine since implementing the programme, it has come close. On 8 January 2005 the SSN USS *San Francisco* collided with a large undersea seamount 350 nautical miles (650 km) south of Guam in the Marianas Islands. The impact was so severe, with everything not tied down flying forward, that one crew member was killed and 97 were injured. The collision brought the *San Francisco* to an abrupt stop from a speed of 25 knots, collapsed a part of its bow and ruptured its forward ballast tanks, nearly causing the submarine to sink. Only a desperate struggle to maintain buoyancy prevented total catastrophe.

On 21 March 2007 an explosion occurred in the forward section of the British nuclear submarine HMS *Tireless*, killing two crew members. The *Tireless* was on patrol in the Arctic at the time and had to make an emergency surface through pack ice in order for a crew member who had sustained injuries to be airlifted off the submarine. The explosion appeared to have been caused by faulty air-purification equipment and bad maintenance, although full details were withheld.

One crucial factor in determining the cause of submarine accidents is the distinctive psychology of the submariner, a psychology examined by a report from the u.s. Naval Submarine Medical Research Laboratory (NSMRL) on the health issues associated with serving on nuclear submarines. These include the 'psychopathological effects of isolation, increased auditory and visual skills requirements, and a host of human factors problems associated with complex nuclear technology'. The report concluded that the primary problems associated with long submerged patrols include 'obscure symptomology such as headaches, blurred vision, dizziness, malaise, and performance decrements', all of which could lead to 'morale deterioration . . . and, in some cases, debilitative psychopathology'.[7]

The NSMRL found that unless nuclear submarine crew received regular 'periscope liberty' (that is, that ratings be granted, once every 24 hours, a few seconds of periscope viewing of the sea, land, birds in flight and so on), morale dipped. It is one reason why u.s. submarines, weather and mission permitting, let the crew have 'steel beach' parties on the hull, during which they barbecue steaks and dive into the sea. This 'cognitive anchor' to the world beyond the submarine is essential if performance and psychological stability are to be maintained on long missions without surfacing.[8] While the cause of the accidents that befell the *Thresher* and *Scorpion* may have been faulty technology or construction, mistakes by a tired crew denied a cognitive anchor for too long cannot be ruled out.

The NSMRL report also cited an earlier research project, conducted in the 1960s, which had discovered a 'sharp increase in the belligerent attitudes of u.s. Navy submariners following the Cuban Crisis of 1962'.[9] The belligerence would have arisen mainly from the Cold War climate of the time, but also from an atmosphere of suspicion and paranoia created by long-duration missions in which most of the crew were

Logo of the u.s. Navy's Submarine Learning Center in Groton, Connecticut.

kept in ignorance of developments in the outside world.

A submarine's crew is forced by circumstance to re-create the routines and pleasures of onshore civilian life. During the 1960s the American SSN *Growler* had a schedule of social events to emulate life on shore. The crew's mess had a film projector and a different film would be screened every few nights. When not watching a film, the crew held a 'casino night'. They amused themselves by growing beards and comparing each other's efforts. But it was impossible to disguise the fundamental lack of normality of their situation. None of the men took showers, as there was not enough fresh water, or wore pyjamas, instead simply sleeping in their work clothes.[10]

Life on board a modern nuclear-powered submarine offers more comforts, but not many more. Most SSNs and SSBNs have reliable hot-water showers and the standard of cooking in the messes is remarkably high, but although working routines vary across national navies the standard 'day' for submarine crews is an eighteen-hour rotating schedule consisting of six hours on duty, six hours of free time and six hours of sleep. The artificiality of the schedule allied to the lack of the usual signifiers for keeping track of time – dawn, daylight, dusk, night – can be disorientating for the crew. A crew's social life revolves around the 'mess halls', divided by junior ratings, senior ratings and officers.

Although submarine crews can and do find solace and comradeship in each other and in a recreated social life for the duration of a mission, these are the pleasures of inmates, the pastimes of a locked-down family group who cannot leave each other's company or go elsewhere. They only serve to emphasize a perennial theme in the story of the submarine – that of its isolation, its loneliness, its *apartness*. This theme is most heavily articulated in tales of submarine accident and disaster. When crippled and lost, no military vessel is so far from home or more difficult to retrieve than a submarine.

Outside of drama and fiction, submarine accidents rarely result in a dramatic rescue attempt, because total destruction and loss of life is so swift and immediate. There is no military vessel or mode of

Sailors assigned to Los Angeles-class fast-attack submarine USS *Olympia* participate in a swim call at sea in the Pacific Ocean, July 2018.

transport so routinely cut loose from its fellows than a submarine. Once it has deep dived, its satellite connectivity is patchy to non-existent. An SSN or SSBN will still need to rise to periscope depth (that is, shallower than 18 metres (60 ft) below), so that its periscope can rise above surface level to send emails or receive communications. U.S. submarines can request extra satellite bandwidth from the U.S. Navy to send a video or larger data file but the powerful 'spot beams' used for this are reserved for emergencies and important messages only.

Even the most advanced twenty-first-century SSBN can still find itself almost blind. On 4 February 2009 the British SSBN HMS *Vanguard* and the French SSBN *Le Triomphant* collided with each other in the Atlantic while on routine patrols. Both submarines sustained damage although there were no injuries or radioactive leaks. Incredibly, although the UK and France are NATO allies, neither navy was aware of allied submarines in the area, and both were using passive sonar (listening only) not active sonar (emitting pulses and therefore more detectable). Only the submarines' very slow speed prevented more serious damage and the loss of one or both of them.

The submarine and its ambivalent relationship with the surface world is a portrait in miniature of the wider suspicion and mistrust that follows from military posturing between superpowers. Nothing demonstrated this process more starkly than the NATO military exercise Able Archer 83 in November 1983. A massive deployment of NATO land, sea and air forces, the exercise simulated a military confrontation between NATO and the Soviet Bloc that would climax in DEFCON I, when full nuclear obliteration is imminent. Able Archer used new secret codes, radio silences, an unprecedented airlift of 19,000 soldiers from the USA to Europe and (for the first time) the participation of heads of government.

It appears not to have occurred to NATO planners that the Soviet Union might perceive this as the beginning of a real firststrike and respond in kind. Nuclear bombers in East Germany and Poland were placed on high alert and Soviet ICBM silos were opened and primed to fire. With u.s. silos then priming in response, the exercise suddenly morphed into frightening reality. It is now accepted that Able Archer brought the world closer to nuclear war than it had been at any time since the Cuban Missile Crisis.[11]

It was this process that the Marxist historian E. P. Thompson dissected in his remarkable essay 'Notes on Exterminism' (1980), an attempt to analyse the political challenges posed to socialists by the Second Cold War and the emergence of a large cross-European peace movement. Thompson's analysis stripped bare the psychological and institutional impulses at work behind the nuclear escalation of the period, categorizing them as a uniquely dangerous process he labelled 'exterminism'. Breaking with orthodox Marxism, which holds that political developments are a logical reflection of underlying class interests, he dared to ask:

> But to structure an analysis in a consecutive rational manner may be, at the same time, to impose a consequential rationality upon the object of analysis. What if the object is irrational? What if events are being willed by no single causative historical logic ('the increasingly aggressive military posture of world imperialism', etc.) – a logic which then may be analysed in terms of origins, intentions or goals, contradictions or conjunctures – but are simply the product of a messy inertia?[12]

The irrationality of exterminism has dominated the discourse on the nuclear submarine since the launch of the first SSBN. Every war brings it forth. Just prior to the Falklands War, when it became clear to the British government that Argentina was preparing a military build-up, the commander of the SSN HMS *Splendid*, on patrol in the Atlantic, received a 'Blue Key' message (for the captain's eyes only). The message was an order to return to Faslane immediately and prepare for war. In perfect complement to Nena's hit song '99 Red Balloons' – 'This is what we've waited for; this is it, boys, this is war' – the commander's reaction wallowed in exterminism. 'I had waited my whole life for one of these,' he explained. 'It was wonderful.'[13]

The commanders of the UK's four SSBNs wait all their lives for an even more important message, the 'Letters of Last Resort', four identically worded handwritten letters from the British prime minister containing orders on what action to take in the event that an enemy nuclear strike has incapacitated the British government. The letters are stored inside a safe in the control room of each submarine and are destroyed unopened when a prime minister leaves office.

The letters, along with the prime minister's personal authentication codes for the Nuclear Operations Targeting Centre several levels beneath the Ministry of Defence Main Building in Whitehall, are an essential part of the procedures required to launch the UK's nuclear weapons. Writing of this bureaucracy of mass murder, Hennessy and Jinks record, with approval, that 'New Prime Ministers are swiftly indoctrinated into its instruments and procedures.'[14]

The Letters of Last Resort give what will be the final orders of Her Majesty's Government to its SSBN commanders. They specify one of four options – retaliation against the enemy with nuclear weapons; no retaliation; leaving the decision to the commander of the submarine; or an order to place the SSBN under the command of an allied power (probably the U.S.). Since at least one Vanguard-class SSBN is always fully armed and on active service, and each one carries sixteen Trident-II intercontinental ballistic missiles, the Letter of Last Resort is capable of unleashing Armageddon on the enemy country, resulting in mutual annihilation.

The U.S. Navy operates to the same murderous logic. Tom Clancy's genius was to take this logic, filter it through Reaganite ideology and produce the founding texts of the modern techno-thriller. His second book, *Red Storm Rising*, co-authored with Larry Bond, was even more influential than his first. Set in the real world of 1986, it describes in great strategic detail how a Third World War – although one fought, improbably, without ultimate recourse to nuclear weapons – might unfold.

Red Storm Rising has a Soviet Union under threat of economic collapse risk everything on a bold incursion into western Europe, Scandinavia and Iceland. Extrapolating a scenario of conflict between Warsaw Pact and NATO countries on a number of different fronts, including in the North Atlantic where the nuclear submarine USS *Challenger* holds back a Soviet naval attack, Clancy's novel was used as a teaching text at the U.S. Naval War College and influenced the thinking of a generation of American military planners. After the 1986 Reykjavík summit between President Reagan and Mikhail Gorbachev, Reagan recommended Margaret Thatcher read *Red Storm Rising* for an insight into Soviet aims and intentions.

Clancy's work dealt with the global struggle between the USA and USSR with the utmost seriousness. But the irrationality and paranoia of the Cold War, of a nuclear logic literally called MAD, was crying out to be satirized. One of the earliest attempts to do so, Stanley Kubrick's *Dr. Strangelove* (1964), hit its targets savagely and repeatedly, although it focused not on the navy but the air force. Forty years later, the BBC Radio 4 comedy series *Deep Trouble* (2005–7) targeted not the Cold War per se but the submarine genre as exemplified by *The Hunt for Red October*. Set on the British nuclear submarine HMS *Goliath*, it took the modern submarine thriller and stripped it of all dignity. Written by Perrier Award-winner Ben Willbond, its characters are short-sighted idiots more interested in food, promotion and sex than any mission they might have. One is actually named Tom Clancy.

Even *Doctor Who* commented on the absurdity of MAD in the 1980s. In the 2013 episode 'Cold War', written by Mark Gatiss, the eleventh Doctor (Matt Smith) and his companion Clara (Jenna Coleman) find themselves in 1983, at the time of Able Archer, on a Russian SSBN, where the Ice Warrior Skaldak attempts to destroy humanity by firing the submarine's nuclear missiles at America. Although the Doctor defeats the plan by appealing to Skaldak's better nature, Clara is appalled at the alacrity with which both sides in the Cold War are ready to unleash a nuclear holocaust.

Denzel Washington and Gene Hackman in *Crimson Tide* (1995, dir. Tony Scott).

There is a strong argument that satirical polemic is the only appropriate response to MAD, Able Archer and the entire psychopathology of exterminism. Satire denies it dignity, rejects its militaristic, acronym-laden pomposity and allows other, more directly political attacks to take hold. It creates space for dissent and scepticism about the role of the nuclear submarine in the post-Cold War world. Tony Scott's *Crimson Tide* (1995), a film that went for the jugular of the genre with breathtaking audacity, was a significant milestone in that critical process.

Crimson Tide is a tightly scripted chamber piece circling around two strong but contrasting personalities, the conservative traditionalist Captain Ramsey (Gene Hackman) and his new, liberal XO Commander Hunter (Denzel Washington). Set immediately after the fall of the Soviet Union, the film begins with Russian separatists seizing an ex-Soviet nuclear missile site in Chechnya. Sent to patrol the region, the U.S. SSBN *Alabama* receives an EAM (emergency action message, or order to fire nuclear weapons) ordering the immediate launch of its missiles against the installation. Just before it can do so a second EAM is received but is cut off by the surprise attack of a Russian submarine loyal to the separatists, which damages the *Alabama*'s communications. Ramsey wishes to proceed with the launch but Hunter believes the second order may be a retraction and that they should clarify before firing. Ramsey tries to replace Hunter, who instead removes him from command for not following correct procedures.

Crimson Tide directly addresses themes hitherto only implicit within the genre, specifically the nature and purpose of the nuclear submarine. The most compelling detail is that of the authentication procedure for firing nuclear missiles should the submarine receive an EAM, a procedure taken verbatim from the U.S. Navy's Command and Control System,[15] and its reliance on complete unity of command to function. Yet early scenes in the officers' mess establish that captain and XO have different perspectives on warfare and military discipline. The disagreements are so serious that, after a spat in the control room about whether to abandon a fire drill after a submariner is injured, Ramsey takes Hunter to his cabin to tell him: 'We train these boys to do a terrible and unthinkable thing. The only reason they can do it is their unquestioning faith in a unified chain of command. That means they hear your voice ringing out right after mine.'

The crisis throws a spotlight on class and race. In early scenes Hunter is shown talking to and showing respect for enlisted men who work on departments of the submarine – sonar, radio – which are later critical to helping him run the boat under duress. The *Alabama*'s Black crew members primarily side with Hunter. Most of the white junior officers go with Ramsey, but not the veteran Chief of the Boat (the COB – the senior enlisted man), who is appalled that Ramsey jettisons protocol to replace his XO. Hunter, a highly successful, educated Black professional, is instinctively distrusted by Ramsey, and for that reason. 'Excuse me, *Harvard*?' the captain asks, surprised, on reading Hunter's CV.

At one point, before their differences escalate from political philosophy to fighting over the launch keys, Hunter bluntly tells Ramsey, 'In the nuclear age, the real enemy is war itself.' Yet despite its overt critique of exterminism, *Crimson Tide* ultimately loses its nerve. At the last it swerves away from Armageddon and thereby reasserts the under-lying rationality of existing procedures. They were tested to destruction but were not destroyed. But the logic of the EAM procedures could just as easily – much more easily – signal blind obedience and the launching of the doomsday weapons.

It is no surprise that the submarine is often present at, and after, the end of the world, circling a devastated Earth with nowhere to go. *On the Beach* showed a submarine's crew committing suicide in the ruins. In the very different *Terminator Salvation* (dir. McG, 2009),the centre of humanity's resistance to Skynet, the worldwide AI that sends forth the Terminators, resides in the only remaining nuclear submarine left functioning after Judgement Day. Eventually it too is destroyed.

Sometimes the submarine is the last big hitter left in a new world. Brian Wood's award-winning comic *The Massive* (2012–14) is set in a 'post-crash, post-everything' world whose resonance with our own increases with every passing year. One of the new societies seeking to survive, the independent city-state Moksha, is formed of a dozen inter-connected oil rigs and protects itself by keeping an armed ex-Soviet SSBN docked at its side.

Neal Stephenson's ambitious SF novel *Seveneves* (2015) has nuclear submarines literally restarting a new branch of humanity after an explo-sion on the Moon causes an exponential cascade effect, creating a 'hard rain' of debris that wipes out human civilization. Some escape on a 'Cloud Ark' of space habitats, while others flee underground or to the bottom of ocean trenches in submarines. After an audacious 5,000-year time-jump, the novel follows the descendants of those who took dif-ferent paths to survival, including the 'Pingers', long adapted to life at the bottom of the ocean in a string of submarines.

In these cases the submarine is a refuge and a saviour in an environ-ment grown harsh and cold. By contrast, in the American TV series *The Last Ship* (2014–18) a nuclear submarine is the most dangerous antag-onist to the last surviving part of the U.S. Navy, the destroyer USS *Nathan James*, after a global pandemic wipes out 80 per cent of the

world's population. When the heroic crew of the *Nathan James*, with
the help of a brilliant virologist, develop a vaccine, they are opposed
by home-grown fascists quite content with the fallout of power and a
group of fundamentalist 'Immunes' who have taken control of a British
SSN and use it to impose their will.

PC games have also tapped into fashionable 'end of the world' narratives. In 2017, in the tradition of the highly successful video game of
Clancy's *Red Storm Rising*, another Cold War-era submarine simulation game, *Cold Waters*, was released on Steam for PC and MacOS. In
the game the lead player commands a U.S. SSN in one of a series of
hypothetical Third World Wars that break out in either 1968, 1984 or
2000, depending on which alternate reality is chosen. The sub-sim
game *AquaNox* jumps forward to 2661, after mankind has ruined Earth
in a series of wars over its dwindling natural resources. Humanity then
lives in underwater cities divided into various power blocs protected
by technologically advanced submarines, the missions of which drive
the game.

It is not difficult to extrapolate a doomsday scenario from the current state of international relations. After a brief interval when the SALT
and START treaties put caps on new weapon systems and oversaw the
decommissioning of old ones, the era of Trump and Putin has seen a
reversion to military escalation. The Trump administration's decision
in October 2018 to cease compliance with the Intermediate-Range
Nuclear Forces (INF) Treaty, citing Russia's production of a new generation of nuclear missiles that it claimed violated the treaty, signalled
that the era of even nominal arms control was over.[16]

Taking full advantage of the new freedom, the USA is now mass-
producing a new iteration of nuclear weapon known as the W76-2. This
is a variant of the Navy's primary submarine-launched nuclear weapon,
the W76-1, which has a yield of around 100 kilotons (the bomb dropped
on Hiroshima had a yield of about 15 kilotons).[17] Aware that it cannot
match America in number and yield of nuclear weapons, Russia is put-
ting its faith in more flexible delivery systems, including the 'Status-6

Oceanic Multi-Purpose System', a nuclear-powered and nuclear-armed unmanned submersible developed by the Rubin Corporation, Russia's top-secret centre of submarine design.

The Status-6 is able to deliver a thermonuclear cobalt bomb of up to 200 megatons against an enemy's naval ports and coastal cities. In January 2019 it was reported that the Russian Navy will order over thirty Status-6 underwater drones, deployed on at least four submarines, to be available by 2027. The USA would of course deploy its SSNs, on high alert and ready to fire, against any such perceived incursion.[18]

America's SSNs, its feared fast-attack submarines, continue to gear up for conflict, not all of it on a global or intercontinental level. The SSN, because of its speed, stealth and manoeuvrability, is often envisaged as being an aid to much smaller operations. A report in *Wired* magazine on a tour of duty by USS *Mississippi* recorded:

> There's a special bay, called a lockout trunk, that allows a tinier sub to dock and deposit a small number of SEALs onboard. Once they're aboard, the *Mississippi* will become a Navy special warfare platform – as are many subs that don't carry nuclear missiles – performing reconnaissance missions and getting SEALs stealthily in and out of where they need to go. The Virginia class's smaller size allows the sub to 'be more maneuverable in a littoral,' says Master Chief Bill Stoiber, the chief of the boat, or senior enlisted man aboard, making it particularly useful for SEAL insertion missions.[19]

At the same time, the U.S. Navy is accelerating development and construction of its new Columbia-class SSBNs to ensure it possesses the most lethal, high-tech ballistic missile submarines possible. These will enter service by 2031 and serve into the 2080s. The new submarines are being designed for 42 years of service life with a 'life-of-ship' reactor core that negates mid-life refuelling. Once complete, this programme would enable the U.S. Navy to build twelve new

SSBNs with the same sea presence as the current fleet of fourteen Ohio-class SSBNs.

Yet the prosaic reality is that the nuclear submarine will not outlive the end of human civilization. Although SSNs and SSBNs have a good chance of surviving a nuclear war and the immediate fallout (water is an excellent defence against radiation), and while their nuclear reactors could, in theory, give them locomotive power for about thirty years, they would run out of food in about six months. Surfacing to resupply would expose them to the hazards they had previously avoided, to say nothing of the collapse of its crew's military discipline from the knowledge that their country and loved ones were all gone.

The lonely fate of USS *Sawfish* in *On the Beach*, last survivor of a conflagration for which it is partly responsible, remains the ultimate in submarine nihilism. As Captain Nemo memorably warned in the genre's founding text, 'The globe begins with the sea, and who is to say it will not end with it?'

4

THE SUBMARINE AS EXPLORER

The prototype submarines developed by David Bushnell, Robert Fulton and Brutus de Villeroi were designed for military use, but the submarine has always had immense utility for scientific research and exploration. Although the depiction of the submarine in popular culture is inextricable from stories of war, Jules Verne's *Twenty Thousand Leagues Under the Sea* is about an independent exploratory vessel owned and captained by a civilian inventor, Captain Nemo. The bulk of its narrative centres on the beauty of the ocean and the seabed, on marine biology and ecology.

The influence of Verne's classic on all aspects of subsequent maritime exploration is beyond dispute. The name of the international trade union for seafarers – whose membership includes shipmasters, officers and ratings, yacht crew, river boatmen, harbour masters, nautical college lecturers and ship-based medical personnel – is Nautilus International. Similarly, the Nautilus Institute for Security and Sustainability, a trans-national public policy think tank, founded in 1992, conducts research on 'strategies to solve interconnected global problems. With networks of partners, we develop and apply these strategies to the linked threats of nuclear war, urban and energy insecurity, and climate change in the Asia Pacific region.' Verne, and of course Nemo, would approve.

Verne's non-military themes remain the prophetic core of the genre, part of an intellectual tradition stretching from Leonardo da Vinci to

Édouard Riou,
illustration of the
crew on the back of
the submarine boat,
from Jules Verne,
*Vingt mille lieues
sous les mers* (1871).

Alphonse de Neuville, 'A window opened into this unexplored abyss', illustration from Jules Verne, *Vingt mille lieues sous les mers* (1871).

Arthur C. Clarke. This legacy encompasses heterodox thinkers such as John Wilkins, Bishop of Chester in the seventeenth century, whose astounding range of speculative work included *The Discovery of a New World; or, A Discourse Tending to Prove, that 'tis Probable There May be Another Habitable World in the Moone: With a Discourse Concerning the Possibility of a Passage Thither* (1638). Wilkins's later treatise on future technology, *Mathematical Magick; or, The Wonders That May be Performed by Mechanicall Geometry* (1648), includes essays on the feasibility of flying machines and submarines, ideas which formed the basis for later experiments in submersible design by Bushnell and Fulton in the eighteenth and early nineteenth centuries.

In 1864 the French submarine *Plongeur*, the first to be propelled by mechanical rather than human power, began underwater trials in La Rochelle harbour. Despite a revolutionary compressed air engine with 23 tanks of air to work it, the boat collided with the quay. Although it was decommissioned in 1872, the *Plongeur* announced the arrival of the submarine in popular culture. In 1867 a model of the *Plongeur* was exhibited at the second International Exposition in Paris, where it was closely studied by Verne. In 1870 *Twenty Thousand Leagues Under the Sea* was published, and was such an immediate success that it was followed a year later by an illustrated edition with over a hundred superbly detailed illustrations by the French artists Édouard Riou and Alphonse de Neuville. It has never since been out of print.

Verne worked with the history given to him. Born in 1828, by the time he produced *Twenty Thousand Leagues* he had already established his reputation as the author of *Journey to the Centre of the Earth* (1864) and *From the Earth to the Moon* (1865). In *Twenty Thousand Leagues* he introduced not only the first, best and consummate icon of the submarine in literature, the *Nautilus*, but one of the great anti-heroes of popular fiction, Captain Nemo.

Twenty Thousand Leagues is more an oceanographic travelogue than an adventure, an underwater version of *Around the World in Eighty Days*. The main plot beats – the naval expedition to find the aquatic 'beast' that is sinking ships in the Atlantic, followed by the adventures of Professor Aronnax, his assistant Conseil and master harpooner Ned Land on board that beast, the fantastic submarine *Nautilus* – are essentially bookends to an exploration of the submarine itself, and the equally miraculous oceans and seas that it traverses in the course of the story (20,000 leagues is a distance, not a depth).

Verne gives his readers a virtual technical schematic of the *Nautilus*. Nemo explains to Professor Aronnax that it is 'exactly 232 feet, and its maximum breadth is 26 feet', and goes on to provide its weight, the design of its hull and bulkheads, how much water it displaces when submerged and its means of propulsion. For a novel written in 1870, its description of the *Nautilus*'s hydroplanes, by which it controls the angle of ascent and descent, is at the cutting edge of submarine technology, an extrapolation of genius that pre-dated Holland's real-world application of the concept.

Verne consciously eschewed the imaginative leaps found in the science fiction of H. G. Wells. *The Time Machine* (1895) and *The War of the Worlds* (1898) do not provide a scientific explanation for how the time machine or the Martians' deadly heat ray actually work. Comparing his approach to that of Wells, Verne wrote, 'I have always made a point in my romances of basing my so-called inventions upon a ground work of actual fact, and of using in their construction methods and materials which are not entirely without the pale of contemporary engineering skill and knowledge.'[1]

Nemo boasts to Aronnax that he has transcended modern science. 'You have carried out your work as much as terrestrial science permitted you,' he tells the oceanographer he has taken as his prisoner/guest on the Nautilus. 'But you do not know all – you have not seen all. Let me tell you then, Professor, that you will not regret the time passed on board my vessel. You are going to visit the land of marvels.' And so they do, attaining ocean depths never before imagined, encountering undiscovered sea creatures and observing the transatlantic telegraph cable and the ruins of Atlantis.

But the greatest mystery, never entirely solved, is Captain Nemo himself. In Verne's later sequel to *Twenty Thousand Leagues*, the lesser-known *The Mysterious Island* (1874), it is revealed that Nemo is in fact a Muslim Indian prince, Armitage Ranjit Dakkar, who was driven to build the *Nautilus* and sink the ships of colonial nations as revenge for the murder of his wife and children by the British. Despite this being literary canon direct from Jules Verne himself, it was not until 2003, in the otherwise disappointing film adaptation of Alan Moore's graphic novel *The League of Extraordinary Gentlemen*, that Nemo was played by a non-white actor, Naseeruddin Shah.

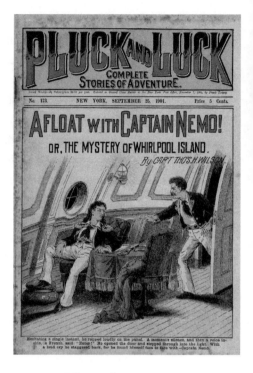

Cover of *Pluck and Luck*, no. 173 (25 September 1901), featuring the story 'Afloat with Captain Nemo! Or, The Mystery of Whirlpool Island', attributed to Cap't Tho's. H. Wilson.

This social and ethnic backstory is entirely absent from *Twenty Thousand Leagues*, where Nemo's motivation is kept deliberately enigmatic. What is clear is that he nurses a great hatred for Western society and for modern civilization in general. In his most imperishable statement, he tells Aronnax,

> The sea is the last reservoir of nature. The globe begins with sea, so to speak, and who knows if it will not end with it? In its supreme tranquility, the sea does not belong to despots. Upon its service men can still exercise unjust laws, fight, tear one another to pieces, and be carried away with terrestrial horrors. But at thirty feet below its level, their reign ceases, their influence is quenched, and their power disappears.

Nemo even has visions of independent, self-sustaining communities living in harmony with nature. 'I can imagine the foundations of

Two of the divers seemed determined to take the life of a third, "My!" thought Frank, "they would kill him!" He made signs to Pomp. The darky pulled his ax from his belt, and, with Frank, started to the rescue.

Cover of *Frank Reade Weekly Magazine*, no. 20 (13 March 1903), featuring the story 'Around the World, Under Water; Or, The Wonderful Cruise of a Submarine Boat', attributed to NoName.

nautical towns, cluster of submarine houses, which, like the *Nautilus*, ascend every morning to breath air at the surface of the water, free towns, independent cities.'² Nemo's flight from nineteenth-century capitalist civilization and his impassioned cry for a radical, ecological alternative make him one of the earliest fictional eco-warriors, a man who uses the submarine not to secure military and strategic advantage over rival powers but to escape all of them.

Nemo and his *Nautilus* are an anomaly at the heart of the submarine genre. As developed between 1870 and the early twenty-first century, the genre is almost inextricable from the trope of imperialistic navies vying for dominance over vital strategic regions through superior firepower. The *Red October* is hunted by the USA and USSR for its ability to alter the balance of global power. It has no other rationale. But Verne's novel, the first and arguably greatest submarine story ever written, exhibits none of these concerns, except to reject them.

Twenty Thousand Leagues was an immediate and enduring success, producing multiple spin-offs. The popular early twentieth-century American pulp magazine *Pluck and Luck (Complete Stories of Adventure)* published a story in which Sam Clemens (Mark Twain) is kidnapped by the *Nautilus* and encounters Captain Nemo. Not willing to pay for the copyright, the equally popular *Frank Reade Weekly Magazine* serialized a story called 'Around the World Under Water; or, The Wonderful Cruise of a Submarine Boat', by 'No Name'. Regardless of these stories' pedigree, readers lapped them up.

In 1916 Verne's novel was made into a film using revolutionary undersea film techniques. In order to use the clearest seawater, it was filmed off the coast of the Bahamas, and provided audiences of the day a unique glimpse of oceanic life. But it was the 1954 Walt Disney version, with James Mason as Captain Nemo, that left an indelible imprint on the popular memory. The scientists in Michael Crichton's *Sphere* (1987), trapped in an underwater habitat, share recollections of watching the Disney adaptation, remembering Mason's Nemo and Kirk Douglas's Ned Land clearly, but failing to recall who played Aronnax.

The 1954 film jettisoned most of the marine ecology, which made up three-quarters of Verne's narrative, for a colourful proto-steampunk adventure. There is a fitful attempt to make the boorish Ned Land the hero, but Land remains a buffoon aptly characterized by Nemo as a man who could commit a good deed one day and reverse it the next. Nemo, immortalized by a dignified but tortured Mason, dominates him and the movie in every way.

Walt Disney, a fellow creative megalomaniac, could not hide his admiration for Nemo or for the *Nautilus*, which was lovingly crafted and filmed. It had outstanding production design and technical effects (the film won Oscars for Best Art Direction and Best Special Effects), and the film's *pièce de resistance* was the model and interior set design of the *Nautilus*, which established an iconic template for steampunk

Poster for *20,000 Leagues Under the Sea* (dir. Richard Fleischer, 1954).

submarines that has arguably been more influential than Verne's original conception. In Disney's adaptation it glided serenely through the
ocean depths, fishing the seabed for delicious delicacies and occasionally
sinking slave ships.

H. G. Wells's short story 'In the Abyss' (1896) merged Verne's
scientism with visionary fantasy. Wells has his inventor hero, Elstead,
descend to the uncharted depth of 8 kilometres (5 mi.) below the surface of the ocean in a prototype bathysphere (which in reality only
began to be used in the 1930s), where he encounters a civilization of
human-fish hybrid creatures. The creatures take him to their city and
prostrate themselves before him, as for a god fallen from heaven. Elstead
eventually returns to the surface, but after a further descent is not
seen again.

Both Verne and Wells imagined vessels and devices – *Nautilus*, the
time machine, Elstead's bathysphere – that did not and perhaps could
not exist. By contrast, Edgar Rice Burroughs's fantasy *The Land That
Time Forgot* (1918) simply employed the submarine of its day. By 1918
Burroughs had established himself as a master of pulp fantasy, with his
first *Tarzan* novels and the beginning of the 'Pellucidar' series, including *At the Earth's Core* (1914). In the 1920s he cemented that reputation
with the full development of several fictional mythos, including Tarzan
and John Carter of Mars. *The Land That Time Forgot*, a novella originally entitled 'The Lost U-boat', was the first of his 'Caspak' series, to
be followed by *The People That Time Forgot* and *Out of Time's Abyss*.

Burroughs's story, set during the First World War, follows the adventures of Bowen Tyler, an American shipbuilder and manufacturer of
submarines who before the war had supplied them to the USA, France,
Britain and Germany. Burroughs may have been slighting the ease with
which the Electric Boat Company, the precursor of General Dynamics,
had before the war sold submarines to Germany, Japan and Russia as
well as the USA and Britain.

There is deliberate irony, therefore, when Tyler is among those on
a civilian liner in the Atlantic torpedoed by a U-boat. He and a small

group of survivors, including an American woman, Lys La Rue, are
accidentally picked up by the *U-33*, whereupon they hijack the submarine. Through a series of misadventures the *U-33* lands on the
undiscovered island of Caprona, a unique, prehistoric ecosystem that
is home to dinosaurs, pterodactyls and a variety of primitive cavemen
at differing stages of physical and cultural evolution.

Written at the close of the First World War, *The Land That Time
Forgot* was perfectly placed to reflect Anglo-American attitudes towards
U-boats. In the first few pages Bowen tells the reader, 'We were aboard
an American ship – which, of course, was not armed. We were entirely
defenseless; yet, without warning, we were being torpedoed.'³ Once
the survivors are on board the *U-33*, Burroughs makes it clear that the
German crew, led by ruthless aristocrat Baron von Schoenvorts, are
devious and unreliable. Although the survivors and the crew are forced

Poster for *The Land
That Time Forgot*
(dir. Kevin Connor,
1974).

to work together on Caprona, at the first chance they get the Germans take the submarine and abandon the others to their fate.

The 1975 film adaptation reflects changed times and attitudes. Directed by Kevin Connor, its screenplay is by the polymathic fantasy novelist Michael Moorcock, a writer perfectly suited to adapt Burroughs's Edwardian derring-do. In Moorcock's version, the captain of the *U-33* (John McEnery) is sympathetic, scientifically literate and interested in the ecology of Caprona. His first officer, Dietz, takes the role of the merciless German keen to surface the submarine and machine-gun the survivors of their attack, a request the captain refuses.

Realizing its special effects would not aid suspension of disbelief, the film delays arrival at Caprona to nearly halfway through. Up to that point it is a grey and gritty First World War adventure (leaving aside the captain's hyper-civilized cabin with its large desk, bookshelf and drinks cabinet, luxuries no U-boat captain ever possessed), with a stern Doug McClure leading the survivors to take over the *U-33*. Once stranded on Caprona, the *U-33* is central to the narrative, and its sinking as the Germans in it try to escape – Deitz having shot the captain and abandoned Bowen and Lys – seals their fate and ends the story, save the message in a bottle thrown into the sea that bookends both the novel and the film.

In placing the submarine at the centre of a rich, imaginative fantasy, Burroughs came both too soon and too late. Two world wars, and the ruthless use of the submarine to strike at enemy shipping including merchant and civilian vessels, had to pass into history before Verne's original conception of a submersible that bears explorers to the edges and depths of the world could fully revive.

Earth's oceans and seas are environments as hostile to human explorers as outer space. At depths below 1,000 metres (3,280 ft), in the so-called 'Midnight Zone', no light penetrates at all. Added to this formidable obstacle, the sheer weight of water prevents deep sea exploration. At the deepest parts of the ocean the pressure level is 1,100 times stronger than at the water's surface. The deepest a scuba diver has ever reached is a mere 318 metres (1,044 ft) down. Below this level humans cannot survive except inside hollow pressure hulls built to withstand the pressure of water at such depths. But even the most robust submarine will implode at its 'crush depth', the depth at which a submarine's structure or hull will suffer total collapse due to the external pressure of water.

For all these reasons the ocean depths remain the final frontier of discovery, a frontier first breached by the 1872–6 expedition of the British scientific research vessel HMS *Challenger*. Redesigned to include extra laboratory and cabin space, dispensing with all but two of its guns to incorporate the material needed for its mission, *Challenger*'s voyage was the first global marine research expedition in history, discovering over 4,000 new marine species and laying the foundations of modern oceanography. Among *Challenger*'s deep-sea soundings was the charting, in March 1875, of the deepest part of the world's oceans, the bottom of the 11-kilometre-deep (36,000 ft or 6 mi.) Mariana Trench between Guam and Palau, subsequently named Challenger Deep.

While twelve humans have stood on the surface of the Moon, as of 2019 only three had ever been to Challenger Deep (in 2020 a series of new descents in the $50-million experimental submersible *Limiting Factor*, led by the private equity investor/undersea explorer Victor Vescovo, took several more people down). In 1960 the U.S. Navy's top-secret Project Nekton sent the Deep Submergence Vehicle (DSV) *Trieste*, crewed by its designer Jacques Piccard and U.S. Navy Lieutenant Don Walsh, to the bottom. It was the first time humanity had reached the deepest parts of the planet. The descent took 4 hours and 47 minutes. At 9 kilometres (30,000 ft) one of the *Trieste*'s outer plexiglass window panes cracked but did not break. It continued its descent and spent twenty minutes in Challenger Deep. In 1963 the *Trieste* was also used in the desperate search for the lost U.S. submarine *Thresher*.

As of 2020 the USA possessed only one vessel devoted to exploring the seabed and ocean crust, the National Oceanic and Atmospheric Administration (NOAA) ship *Okeanos Explorer*. Among other tasks it maps the Pacific Ocean's 100,000 'seamounts', underwater peaks in excess of 1,000 metres (3,300 ft) from the seabed.[4] Although the *Okeanos Explorer* and the research vessel *Atlantis*, owned by the Woods Hole Oceanographic Institute, occasionally deploy manned submersibles, none can venture as deep as the Tridal 2 Hadal Exploration System, a two-person submersible with a 9-centimetre-thick (3.5 in.) titanium hull owned by the private research company Caladan Oceanic.[5]

The relative lack of deep-sea capacity of the manned submarine has not prevented it being used in imaginative narratives of exploration and discovery from Verne onwards. The nearest the U.S. Navy has ever come to realizing this idealistic conception was Research Submersible *NR1*, informally known as 'Nerwin'. Launched in 1969, *NR1* was a 43-metre-long (142 ft) mini-nuclear submarine with a crew of two officers, three enlisted men and two scientists, powered by a custom-built miniaturized nuclear reactor the size of a fridge. Containing no weapons, it used the extra space for advanced computing and electronics technology. It carried out a range of scientific investigations, and in 1986 helped retrieve the wreckage of the space shuttle *Challenger* from the seabed.

A pet project of Admiral Rickover, Nerwin's primary functions were initially underwater search and recovery, oceanographic research and installation of underwater equipment. As the *NR1* was officially never given a name or commissioned, Rickover could spend what he liked on the project without congressional oversight of its operations. Inevitably, despite its immense promise for pure science and exploration, the *NR1* was diverted into Cold War black ops and its voyages to the bottom of the sea were compromised from the start.[6]

The fate of the *NR1* suggests that the U.S. nuclear submarine fleet's only real purpose is to further American military and strategic interests and any other outcome, such as the expansion of scientific knowledge, is an accidental by-product. USS *Triton*, the first twin reactor submarine ever constructed, was launched in 1958. Two years later it was ordered to circumnavigate the globe, tracing Magellan's original route. But this concealed its real mission, which was to obtain reliable gravimetric data from a stable platform (the submerged submarine) to aid the launch of the first U.S. space capsule, a project given the highest political priority since the successful launch of the Soviet Sputnik 1.

During the 1990s and in the first years of the new century the USA began to exploit the 'peace dividend' resulting from the fall of the Soviet Union to experiment with new designs for its SSNs that allowed a greater capacity for scientific research and exploration. The result of this new freedom to experiment were the innovative Seawolf-class attack submarines designed with radical new capabilities – *Seawolf*, *Connecticut* and *Jimmy Carter* – rolled out between 1992 and 2005.

The SSN *Jimmy Carter*, still in use, has a 30-metre-long (100 ft) hull extension called a 'multi-mission platform' (MMP), an underwater hangar that can hold deep-diving remotely operated vehicles (ROVs), custombuilt heavy machinery, special forces supplies and deployable sensors and weapons. Divers, commandos and ROVs can be deployed and recovered through a lockout chamber system built within the MMP. Although perfectly suited for marine exploration, the *Jimmy Carter*, like the *NR1*, has been used primarily for clandestine operations.

The contest between the superpowers over space and territory remains as sharp now as it was during the Cold War. In 2007 Russia staked a claim to the Arctic when two of its mini-submarines, *Mir-1* and *Mir-2*, reached the sea bed more than 4 kilometres (2.5 mi.) beneath the North Pole. In a record-breaking dive the two submarines planted a 1-metre-high (3 ft) titanium Russian flag on the Lomonosov Ridge, which the Russian government claims is directly connected to its continental shelf. It then submitted a claim to the UN for over 1.2 million square kilometres (463,000 square mi.) of sea shelf extending 650 kilometres (350 nautical mi.) from the shore. The claim is part of a battle for jurisdiction over the Arctic, which is believed to contain up to a quarter of the planet's undiscovered oil and gas.

The most positive and potentially beneficial underwater projects of recent decades have been a series of habitable ocean laboratories developed from the 1960s, from the 'Continental Shelf Station Two'

U.S. Navy deep-sea research submersible (bathyscaphe) *Trieste* hoisted out of the water in a tropical port, *c.* 1958–9.

(ConShelf II) project of the undersea explorer Jacques Cousteau to more extensive bases such as that used by NASA's Extreme Environment Mission Operations (NEEMO) project. NEEMO simulates conditions in spaceflight and on Mars by sending astronauts (called 'Aquanauts' for the duration of the missions) to live and work in the Aquarius Reef Base, an underwater habitat on the ocean floor off Key Largo in the Florida Keys.

The 2020s may see a radical expansion of the undersea research habitat. In 2023, work is scheduled to begin on the 'Proteus' station, a collaborative project between the Swiss designer Yves Behar and the Fabien Cousteau Ocean Learning Center. Estimated to be complete by 2025, it will be the world's most advanced underwater scientific research station, a modular lab with a span of over 1,220 metres (4,000 ft) sitting on stilts 18 metres (60 ft) down off the coast of Curaçao in the Caribbean, powered by ocean, solar and wind energy. Proteus will include an underwater greenhouse and pod apartments for visitors. The stations labs and facilities would be leased to government agencies and academic institutions. If its ambitions are realized it could lead to significant advances in marine ecology, medicine, genetics and humanity's understanding of coral reefs and other sub-tidal habitats.

In fiction, the ocean habitat adventure is a tiny niche genre, of which Barry Levinson's *Sphere* (1998), based on Michael Crichton's SF novel, is the clear standout. Both *Sphere* and James Cameron's *The Abyss* (1989) centre on the discovery of what appears to be an alien spaceship at the bottom of the ocean. But although *The Abyss*'s innovative use of CGI received much praise, Cameron's narrative is an unfocused and grandiloquent mess. It never attains its vaulting ambition, preferring *E.T.*-like sentimentality and clichéd personal melodrama to serious engagement with its underlying themes.

Sphere, by contrast, explores the intellectual and psychological challenges of life at the outer edges of humanity's experience. The anomalous object on the sea bed thought to be an alien spacecraft is actually a NASA craft from the future containing a salvaged alien artefact with the power to physically manifest unconscious dreams and desires. Unlike Cameron's working-class oil drillers, hauled from a John Wayne film into a piece of radical science fiction, *Sphere* follows a realistically diverse group of scientists as they explore the alien craft in an underwater habitat reached by mini-submarine.

Naturally their encounter with the sphere goes awry as it conjures their personal demons outside and inside the habitat, the most dangerous of which are drawn from *Twenty Thousand Leagues Under the Sea*, an abiding childhood memory of one of the scientists. When his repressed fear of giant sea creatures is tapped into by the sphere, hundreds of copies of Verne's classic appear throughout the habitat, all blank after a certain page but used as source material to manifest a killer giant squid and lethal jellyfish. Verne's story thus becomes a Freudian id within the genre it gave birth to, a psychic threat that *Sphere*'s characters must transcend in order to survive.

American SF films of the 1950s such as *It Came from Beneath the Sea* (1955) portrayed the nuclear submarine as a helpful scientific tool, instrumental in saving mankind from mutated monsters and other

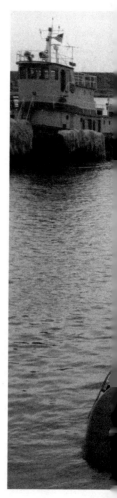

disasters. The hugely successful American TV series *Voyage to the Bottom of the Sea* (1964–8) was that romantic and positive conception of the submarine at full throttle.

The series was developed from a 1961 film of the same name, a stupendously illogical adventure about the prototype submarine *Seaview*. The *Seaview* is the pet project of Admiral Harriman Nelson (Walter Pidgeon), an unlikely hybrid of Rickover and Einstein whose position in the U.S. defence establishment is unclear. The *Seaview* itself, while

The nuclear-powered research submersible *NR-1* as it approaches port, n.d.

it has a conventional military command structure, is referenced throughout as a 'federal' or 'government' vessel, part of the United States Oceanographic Survey (USOS).

The *Seaview* is called upon when the Van Allen radiation belt around Earth catches fire. Leaving aside how this could possibly occur in the absence of oxygen, the effect is that Earth's sky is set ablaze, scorching jungles and forests and melting the polar icecaps. Admiral Nelson's plan to offset this by firing a nuclear missile into the belt from a precise location at an exact time, thus exploding it *away* from Earth, is understandably not accepted by the UN, forcing him to proceed on his own authority. After misadventures and detours the *Seaview* reaches its destination and fires its missile. The plan works, and the celebratory end of the film ignores the irreversible devastation already inflicted on human civilization.

The real star of the film, however, is the *Seaview* itself. With its Raygun Gothic interiors, primary-coloured display units and cheerful buzz-cut crew, it is a gleaming product of William Gibson's 'Airstream Futuropolis', the utopian near-future that never was. Its 'deep ping' sonar sound effect, used in the spacious control room or as background to shots of the submarine at depth, is indelibly associated with the adventures of fictional SF submarines.

The subsequent TV series of *Voyage to the Bottom of the Sea* utilized the film's expensive sets, notably the distinctive central bridge of the *Seaview* complete with wide observation windows (made of what pressure-resistant glass no one could say). Along with producer Irwin Allen's other classic SF television shows *Land of the Giants*, *The Time Tunnel* and *Lost in Space*, it became an icon of 1960s American television. Carefully reclassifying the *Seaview* from a USOS to a SSRN to indicate it was now a military research vessel, the TV series was an underwater *Star Trek* that sanitized and refocused the image of the submarine in the popular imagination.

Aside from self-consciously retro products such as *U-571*, all iterations of the submarine genre try to move forwards. The TV series

Voyage to the
Bottom of the Sea
(1961, dir. Irwin Allen).

SeaQuest DSV (1993–6) was an attempt to update *Voyage to the Bottom of the Sea*, albeit with mixed results. Its first season essays a credible near future, with a global conflict in 2018 between the great powers over deep-sea resources (having exhausted all others) leading to the creation by the United Earth Oceans Organization of the peace-keeping vessel *Seaquest*, a 300-metre-long (1,000 ft) high-speed scientific research submarine designed and captained by Nathan Bridger (Roy Scheider).

The *Seaquest* holds more scientists than military personnel but its primary mission, aided by its 'plasma torpedoes' and a 'bio-skin' hull, is to protect the world's growing number of undersea habitats from mercenaries and corporate pirates. Unfortunately *Seaquest*'s second season lost its nerve and had the submarine encounter aliens buried at the bottom of the ocean, prehistoric monsters and time travel. The ditching of its commitment to a plausible near-future made for an uneven tone and unsatisfactory stories and by its third season, retitled *Seaquest 2032*, its audience had departed.

Seaquest's failure notwithstanding, the idea of life in a submarine still holds broad appeal to a large public. A particular representation of the submarine – Verne's *Nautilus*, or at least Disney's version of it – continues to be packaged for popular consumption and vicarious enjoyment in the 'Tomorrowland' area of Disneyland California.

When Tomorrowland opened in 1955 it used leftover sets from Disney's *20,000 Leagues* as a walk-through attraction and its most popular ride, opening in 1959, was the Submarine Voyage. This simulated a trip on a nuclear submarine, specifically the passage under the North Pole undertaken by USS *Nautilus* in 1954. Being Disney, it added mermaids, a Graveyard of Lost Ships and a visit to Atlantis for good measure. In 1998 the ride was closed for refurbishment, reopening in 2007 as the Finding Nemo Submarine Voyage (that is, Nemo the animated clownfish, not Verne's captain). Along with Space Mountain and the Jedi Training Academy, the Submarine Voyage remains Tomorrowland's premier attraction.

Disneyland provides a commodified and domesticated vision of the real-life oceanographic exploration carried out by the likes of Jacques Cousteau and Robert Ballard. Cousteau's work with the Free French during the war led in 1946 to him being placed in charge of the Underwater Research Group of the French Navy, where he led the exploration of Roman wrecks off the coast of Tunisia. This was the first underwater archaeological mission to fully and properly use

Captain Nemo's submarine attraction in Disneyland Paris, 2007.

autonomous diving, an operation which laid the groundwork for significant advances in marine archaeology.

After leaving the Navy in 1950 Cousteau purchased a former Royal Navy minesweeper, the *Calypso*, and converted it into a mobile oceanographic research and exploratory vessel. In 1956 his film *The Silent World*, made with the French film director Louis Malle and one of the first films to use colour underwater cinematography, won the Palme d'Or at Cannes. He went on to make more than 120 television documentaries on marine life and founded an international brand. As well as revolutionizing modern scuba diving equipment, Cousteau pioneered radical new designs in underwater habitats and mini-submarines.

The TV series *The Undersea World of Jacques Cousteau* (1966–76) made him a household name, such that when the auteur film-maker Wes Anderson made the satirical comedy *The Life Aquatic with Steve Zissou* (2004) it was obvious who and what was being parodied. While Anderson gently mocks the artifice of many of Zissou's filmed exploits, he does not deny him his talent. Zissou (Bill Murray) is an insensitive failure at the domestic and quotidian but rises to emergencies and big occasions. His hunt for the semi-mythical 'jaguar shark' that killed his partner exposes him at his best and worst.

Anderson's weaving of the Brazilian singer-songwriter Seu Jorge's gentle Portuguese versions of David Bowie classics throughout the film catches the plangent effect of Zissou/Cousteau's adventures. After Zissou's meandering journey, including an encounter with a hated rival's high-tech research vessel and Somalian pirates, the only instance of undersea exploration occurs in the final scenes when Zissou's submersible, packed with the supporting characters, finally descends to catch the shark. The descent is surreal and magical, with flashes of animation, as Zissou's colleagues and wife experience the wonders of the deep through his eyes. The film dispenses entirely with marine science as the shark is revealed as a glowing golden creature which Zissou no longer wishes to kill.

Like Cousteau, Robert Ballard started his career as an oceanog- Jacques Cousteau
rapher in his country's navy. After he left the service he worked for the climbing into his
Woods Hole Institute, using ROVs to explore and map the 'Black diving saucer on
board the *Calypso*
Smokers' (hydrothermal vents) of the Mid-Atlantic Ridge. The use of while docked in
mini-submarines and submersibles had been instrumental in the dis- New York Harbor,
covery of hydrothermal vents in 1977, which in turn led to the discovery August 1959.

of new species of 'extremophiles', organisms that feed off the chemicals spewing from the vents. It is a scientific research programme vaguely predicted in the SF film *Around the World Under the Sea* (1966) in which a civilian research submarine, the *Hydronaut*, circumnavigates the world to plant earthquake-monitoring sensors on the ocean floor.

In the 1980s Ballard was chosen to lead the institute's search for the wreck of the *Titanic*, carried out by its research vessel R/V *Knoor*. Aside from Ballard, *Knoor*'s crew were not informed that its mission had been financed by the U.S. Navy on the proviso that it first search for the wreckage of the two U.S. nuclear submarines, *Scorpion* and *Thresher*, which had sunk mysteriously in the 1960s. The Navy considered that Ballard's new ROV, the *Argo*, had the best chance of finding the two lost SSNs, and reactivated his naval commission for the duration of the mission. Only after the *Argo* found the imploded wreckage of the two submarines on the ocean bed did *Knoor* begin to search for the *Titanic*.

On 1 September 1985 the *Argo* found scattered objects on the ocean floor, including a large boiler, a trail which led ultimately to the awesome remains of the *Titanic*, torn in two by the stresses of its upending and sinking. The photographs taken then and later of the dead ship, marooned at a depth of 3,600 metres (12,000 ft) on the ocean floor, assured Ballard's fame. He went on to use the submersibles *Argo* and *Alvin* to discover the wrecks of the *Bismarck* (1989), the *Lusitania* (1993), USS *Yorktown* (1998) and John F. Kennedy's *PT-109* motor torpedo boat (2002).

The discovery of the *Titanic* and the film of its opalescent, encrusted remains sealed its legend in the popular imagination. James Cameron (the third man ever to reach Challenger Deep, in 2012, in the submersible *Deepsea Challenger*) retold the story of its sinking in the multi-Oscar-winning *Titanic* (1997), a crude soap opera in comparison to the less costly but more affecting *A Night to Remember* (1958). The concept of raising the *Titanic* was explored in Clive Cussler's most successful novel, *Raise the Titanic!* (1976), written before Ballard's discovery of the wreck, as part of a convoluted Cold War plot to retrieve a rare mineral ore, the only remaining sample of which is in the *Titanic*'s hold.

Arthur C. Clarke's *The Ghost from the Grand Banks* (1990) was a superior version of the same idea. As with most of Clarke's later work, *The Ghost from the Grand Banks* is less active plot than a series of future studies loosely connected to the theme of raising the *Titanic* on the centenary of its sinking in 2012. Much of the incidental narrative, such as a child prodigy's mastery of fractal theory, goes nowhere. Among the near-future technological marvels Clarke toys with are small 'float glass' spheres attached to the wreck to gently lift it, and the world's only deep-diving tourist submarine, the *Piccard* (named for the inventor of the submersible *Trieste*, and with a lush interior modelled on Verne's *Nautilus*), which takes rich investors down to the *Titanic* to observe the laborious operations.

Crucial to the effort are two decommissioned nuclear submarines bought by the consortium in charge and put to good use by having their reactors run endless power down to the operation on the seabed. In the final twenty pages Clarke remembers that the novel requires an ending, throws in an undersea earthquake that derails the plans developed in the preceding twenty pages and kills a major character in his submersible. The book then concludes, a wry commentary on nature once again shrugging off mankind's hubristic technology.[7]

Clarke's major statement on future marine ecology, *The Deep Range* (1957), written decades before, has the twenty-first-century World Food Organization use atomic power to run huge oceanic plankton farms, 'meadows of the sea', guarded by a fleet of mini-submarines, their only enemy the killer whales that disrupt the farms. With no hint of global warming, beneficent nuclear power plants on the ocean floor and the demise of Christianity and Islam after 'late twentieth-century archeological discoveries' destroy their credibility, *The Deep Range* has not dated well. From the originator of the geo-synchronous orbital satellite and space elevator, it is a benign but clumsy misjudgement, a playful frolic in a sub-aqueous utopia.[8]

Frank Herbert, author of the eco-SF classic *Dune* (1965), suggested a grimmer but more probable future in his earlier work *The Dragon in the Sea* (1956). Set after a limited nuclear exchange between East and West leaves Britain and western Europe devastated, the Western and Eastern Blocs have been at war for ten years and the West is reaching the end of its energy resources. The West's secret weapon is specialized miniature nuclear submarines, called Sub-Tugs, that raid the East's underwater oil fields and drag oil back home in large inflatable tubes attached to the boat (a technology later developed as the 'Dracone Barge' designed to carry liquid cargo submerged behind a ship, and named in homage to Herbert's novel).

Herbert's story follows the Sub-Tug *Fenian Ram* and the mission of psychologist John Ramsey to discover why Sub-Tug crews have started to go insane, exploring not only subterranean warfare but the psychological stresses of long service in small vessels at hazardous depths. 'I'm nuts,' admits one experienced Sub-Tug captain, 'but I'm nuts in a way that fits me perfectly to my world.'[9]

Writing in the mid- to late twentieth century, Herbert and Clarke did not conceive of the submarine's future use in any environment other than Earth's oceans. This is no longer the case. Space exploration in and beyond our solar system may provide a use for remote-operated submarines, and possibly, in interstellar scenarios and exoplanets yet to be encountered, crewed vessels.

NASA's planned missions to Jupiter's moon Europa in the 2030s and Saturn's moon Titan in a more indefinite future envisage heavily adapted, remote-operated submarines exploring the oceans and lakes thought to exist beneath their frozen crusts. However these future submarines may be utilized, it is unlikely to be in the manner envisaged in Harry Harrison's entertaining science fiction novel *The Daleth Effect* (1970), in which a prototype anti-gravity device is simply attached to an existing nuclear submarine, which then doubles as a spacecraft sent to rescue two Soviet cosmonauts stranded on the Moon.

A more immediate and practical use of submariners for exploration beyond Earth's orbit was suggested by the U.S. Naval Institute
(USNI) in 2015 when it recommended that NASA utilize the transferable skills of submarine service crews, in particular their familiarity
with nuclear reactor technology and ability to work in confined spaces
for extended periods. The USNI stated: 'Submariners are the future
of space research'. In conclusion, it was considered that 'Qualified
submariners will thrive as astronauts because of the similarities in the
space and undersea environments. The technical and psychological
experience needed to become a submariner can easily be transferred
to fulfil most of the qualifications of a flight-ready astronaut, allowing
for more streamlined training.'[10]

In the immediate future the best and most progressive use for the
world's submarines remains the fight against climate change. In 2012
the UK's Ministry of Defence (MOD) announced that it would release
the data from its Submarine Estimates of Arctic Turbulence Spectra
(SEATS) project to researchers at the National Oceanography Centre
(NOC). While NOC scientists have previously made trips under the
Arctic aboard UK nuclear submarines in order to measure ice thickness,
these were specific scientific missions. The NOC did not previously have
the benefit of measurements collected as part of standard submarine
operations, information which will help predict how soon the Arctic
will become seasonally ice-free.[11]

The UK's belated release of research data gathered by submarines
is a shadow of a much bigger programme run by the U.S. Navy, the
Submarine Arctic Science Program (originally called the 'Science Ice
Exercise', or SCICEX, an acronym the project retained). Starting in 1993,
SCICEX is an agreement between the U.S. Navy, the National Science
Foundation (NSF), the National Oceanic and Atmospheric Administration (NOAA) and the United States Geological Survey to work
together on specific exercises in which a U.S. submarine carries and
delivers scientific researchers. One of the most important areas of work
conducted as part of the SCICEX projects was to develop a reliable time

USS *Connecticut* submarine and crew members surfacing in the Arctic Circle in Alaska, March 2020.

series to see how rapidly the Arctic's freshwater content and supportive biology are changing under the pressure of climate change.

Annual SCICEX missions took place from 1995 until 1999, when the Navy decided it could no longer put time aside for dedicated scientific missions. To continue the project, the Navy and the marine science community agreed on SCICEX PHASE II, or Science Accommodation Missions (SAMs). Although SAMs do not include civilian scientists on board, time is allocated during otherwise classified submarine exercises for the collection of scientific data. SAMs have been run annually since 2000, with scientists providing the Navy with their research priorities, including measurements of sea ice thickness, ocean hydrography, marine biology and bathymetry.[12] Certain of the submarine's crew are trained in the collection of the data required by scientists and pass it on at the end of the mission.

SCICEX underlined the state-led nature of submarine technology. Simply by virtue of its massive cost, the submarine is hardly ever a civilian or private enterprise. Only with twenty-first-century extremes of personal wealth has the privately owned submarine become possible. For a mere £20 million the Dutch company Ocean Submarine offers its clientele the Neyk Luxury Submarine, an ultra-modern teardrop-shaped design that can carry between ten and twenty passengers and 'aims to bring together the luxury of private jets and super yachts with the latest submersible technology to create the world's first truly high-end personal submarine'.[13]

The larger and most expensive of these 'yacht-submarines' come complete with a sunroof, a helipad and an owner's suite, which can quickly retract and convert to let the submarine descend to depths of 260 metres (850 ft). The purpose is seldom marine exploration. Those who cannot afford to buy an entire submarine can hire, for £175,000 a night, the 'Lovers Deep' luxury submarine promoted by the high-end tour operator Oliver's Travels as 'a service allowing travellers who like to get their thrills between the sheets to get them beneath the waves at the same time'.

Private submarine owners like the Russian oligarch Roman Abramovich share their desire for privacy with Colombian drug cartels, for whom 'narco-submarines', or semi-submersibles, have replaced the Go-Fast Boat as their preferred method of cocaine smuggling. By 2009 the U.S. Drug Enforcement Administration (DEA) had uncovered more than sixty narco-submarines. Although they cost in the region of $2 million to build, the investment is worth it. A single fibreglass diesel-electric narco-submarine can carry enough cocaine in a single trip to generate a $100 million profit for the cartel.

The Marxist insurgency group the Revolutionary Armed Forces of Colombia (FARC) was heavily involved in constructing narcosubmarines for the delivery and sale of cocaine to Mexico's Sinaloa Cartel, the payment for which was used to fund its activities. This activity was discontinued as part of the 2017 Havana Ceasefire Accords between the FARC and the Colombian government, but the use of narco-submarines by other Colombian drug traffickers has intensified, as improved technology allows the submersibles to attain greater depth.[14]

Luxury and narco-submarines demonstrate that the submarine can be whatever its owners make of it. In Kevin Macdonald's film *Black Sea* (2014) it is a technological relic outsourced to corporate capitalism. When veteran Scottish deep-sea salvage expert Robinson (Jude Law) is made redundant and faces unemployment in a post-industrial wasteland, he and his old crew are easy recruits for an anonymous businessman who has learned the location of a Second World War U-boat that was supposedly sunk with a cargo of gold bullion that Stalin was sending to Hitler as part of the Nazi–Soviet Pact. A volatile Scottish–Russian crew is recruited to take an old ex-Soviet diesel-electric submarine from Sevastopol, Crimea, to find the U-boat and retrieve the gold.

From there on *Black Sea* is a Pardoner's Tale under the sea, with the Russian and Scottish submariners falling out over how the gold will be divided. When a catastrophic accident kills half the crew, the

Narco-submarine with a capacity to transport up to 8 tons of cocaine and a sailing range from Colombia to Mexico captured by the Colombian Army in Timbiquí, Department of Cauca, February 2011.

Jude Law in *Black Sea* (2014, dir. Kevin Macdonald).

survivors discover that the company Robinson had worked for had dismissed him and his men as part of a plan to make them desperate for work, pawns it could then rehire through an intermediary and later disavow. Upon discovering the company's plan Robinson attempts to take the damaged submarine and the gold to Turkey, a defiant gesture which does not succeed.

Black Sea is the dark, cynical flipside of submarine exploration, one of the few submarine fictions that dispenses entirely with officers and scientists and puts a non-commissioned, working-class crew at the centre of the drama. The result is their exploitation and betrayal by those who own the means of production. The u.s. Navy and marine ecologists may go exploring but they do so under the umbrella of state and corporate power. Denied that protection, the crew of *Black Sea* are, in every sense, out of their depth.

5

THE SUBMARINE AS FANTASY

The submarine exerts a strange and almost perverse fascination and yet it is not a beautiful or aesthetically pleasing machine. Its conning tower and hydroplanes, like the head and claws of a dinosaur, are vastly out of proportion to its body. Its sleek top hull covers a bulbous underside. It cannot see. It keeps having accidents. Its crews live in absurdly cramped conditions. Despite this, it achieves incredible feats. It goes where no man has gone before. Sometimes it does not return.

The duality of the submarine has long attracted writers of fantasy and the weird. H. P. Lovecraft's short story 'The Temple' (1925), set in 1917, ends in cosmic horror at the bottom of the ocean. After an encounter with a strange talisman that appears to have supernatural properties, the crew of the *U-29* begin to mentally disintegrate, all except its captain, the implacable Von Altberg. But as even he admits, in his last message, 'the circumstances surrounding me are as menacing as they are extraordinary, and involve not only the hopeless crippling of the *U-29*, but the impairment of my iron German will in a manner most disastrous.'[1]

For Lovecraft all human exploration into the unknown was fraught with danger, specifically the existential calamity of glimpsing one's utter insignificance when measured against the scale of the cosmos and the alien entities within it (the 'Great Old Ones' of his Cthulhu mythos). Von Altberg is the only crew member of the *U-29* left alive to see what

Lovecraft hints is the infamous 'corpse-city of R'lyeh', the Cyclopean lost tomb of the Elder God Cthulhu, and to be enticed from the submarine towards the eldritch lights flickering within its pristine Hellenic temple.

In *The Call of Cthulhu* (1928), a longer and richer exploration of his mythos, Lovecraft situates the ruins of lost R'lyeh at 48°52.6's, 123°23.6'w, the exact point in the South Pacific Ocean that is furthest from land in all directions. Known as the Oceanic Pole of Inaccessibility, or 'Point Nemo', the area is now a spacecraft cemetery, which because it has no inhabited locations or maritime traffic is used as a drop zone for hundreds of decommissioned satellites and other dead spacecraft. It is an area only a submarine would and could explore, resonant with ancient and modern ruins, primal shrines and discarded space shuttles, Lovecraft's 'silent secret of unfathomed waters and uncounted years'.[2]

The use of the submarine to transgress boundaries, both physical and spiritual, was exploited in Adam Roberts's astounding philosophical adventure *Twenty Trillion Leagues Under the Sea* (2014). Set in 1954 at the fictional sea trial of France's first nuclear submarine, *Plongeur*, the novel is a dry, ironic homage to Verne's classic. Presented in the formalistic style of a Victorian-era scientific romance, Roberts's story has the *Plongeur* malfunction and plunge to the ocean floor. But it does not crash or implode, instead simply descending endlessly to depths not scientifically possible.

Twenty Trillion Leagues is a postmodernist homage to Verne filtered through the SF of cognitive estrangement. The *Plongeur*'s diving is a falling into ontological chaos as it encounters strange sources of energy and impossible creatures. After a collapse of discipline and morale, the remains of its crew, led by the duplicitous civil servant Lebrain, come to realize that it has somehow passed through a portal, a rent in space-time, into an entirely fluid reality, a 'mini-universe' of water with its own physics and its own Elder God. The *Plongeur* is later revealed to be Jules Verne's *Nautilus* (suitably upgraded), left over from a real history that Verne had presented as fiction.

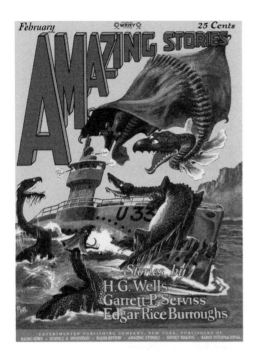

Cover of *Amazing Stories*, February 1927.

Roberts's novel is therefore a continuation of the voyage of the *Nautilus*, although a *Nautilus* subjected to existential dread and loss of identity. Under extraordinary stress, their every scientific certitude crumbling, the apparently stolid crew of the submarine fall apart like a Lovecraftian hero faced with the complete nullity of human civilization, their personalities shattered and reformed in the manner of Jeff VanderMeer or Philip K. Dick. The *Nautilus* is lost for a second time, subverted through the very act of performing its function.[3]

The sheer mimetic force of Verne's creations – Nemo, *Nautilus* – led to their assuming major roles in Alan Moore's pop-cultural epic *The League of Extraordinary Gentlemen*, which brings together iconic protagonists of popular fiction from the nineteenth century (Mina Murray, Allan Quatermain, the Invisible Man, Henry Jekyll/Edward Hyde and Captain Nemo) to form a steampunk Justice League for the British Empire. The League, created by Campion Bond of MI5, first defeat Professor Moriarty and Fu Manchu in London's Limehouse, and later foil the invasion of H. G. Wells's Martians.

Moore fuses all these elements together in an alternate reality with appearances by, or allusions to, an astonishingly large number of characters and situations from mainstream and genre fiction. In the first volume the League discover that 'M', the secret head of MI5, is Professor James Moriarty, who after killing Sherlock Holmes at the Reichenbach Falls ascended to the top of the British secret service while simultaneously constructing a criminal empire in London's West End, his only rival the East End controlled by Fu Manchu. Using cavorite, the material invented by H. G. Wells to power his lunar expedition in *The First Men in the Moon*, Moriarty plans to bombard the East End and destroy his rival.

Nemo and the *Nautilus* are central to the League's efforts to prevent this. Nemo, an autocratic anti-imperialist whose imposing *Nautilus* is a gigantic steampunk engine of death, is a reluctant recruit to the League. Dark-skinned and dressed in regal Sikh uniform, he is explicitly identified as the rebel Indian prince Dakkar. 'Quatermain was always the Empire's favourite son,' Mina tells Nemo. 'You were its nightmare.' 'The winning side writes history books, Miss Murray,' replies a cynical and embittered Nemo.[4]

Moore's main narrative within the *League* series expanded beyond the Victorian era to a linked trilogy, titled *Century*, taking place in 1910, 1969 and 2009, which included a vast array of fictional characters and settings including Duke Prospero, Virginia Woolf's Orlando, A. J. Raffles, *The Threepenny Opera*'s MacHeath, James Bond, Jack Carter of *Get Carter*, Iain Sinclair's Norton (the 'prisoner of London'), Emma Peel, Mick Jagger and Harry Potter. The first part follows Nemo's estranged daughter, Janni Dakkar, who after his death takes up residence in London's Docklands under the name Jenny Diver. When she is gang-raped by local thugs she returns to the *Nautilus* and has it finish the work started by Moriarty in 1898, surfacing in the Thames and annihilating the waterfront to Brecht's lyrics from 'What Keeps Mankind Alive'?

After this Moore develops the story of Janni and the *Nautilus* in three separate stories of their own – *Heart of Ice*, *The Roses of Berlin* and *River of Ghosts* – which are more akin to the original *League* adventures. Janni's decades-long struggle with the evil Ayesha (of H. Rider Haggard's *She*) ends in 1975, in Conan Doyle's Lost World, where a sleek coal-black *Nautilus*, long since stripped of the Gothic frills Captain Nemo had grafted on to it, finally achieves victory and peace of a kind.

The submarine was not always this subtextural. Edward Stratemeyer, the original author of the popular American children's stories of the intrepid boy-inventor Tom Swift – a series which ran from 1910 to its

Poster for *The Atomic Submarine* (dir. Spencer Gordon Bennet, 1959).

last modern incarnation in 2007 – knew that in the years before the First World War the submarine was a source of fascination and wonder for imaginative children. Among the many new inventions and machines that Tom either created or came into contact with in his first series of adventures – such as *Tom Swift and His Motor-Cycle* (1910), *Tom Swift and His Air Glider* (1912) and (an apparent influence on Steve Jobs) *Tom Swift and His Photo Telephone* (1914) – was a submarine, in *Tom Swift and His Submarine Boat* (1910).

Tom Swift would return to the ocean depths many times, most notably in *Tom Swift and His Diving Seacopter* (1956) and *Tom Swift and His Subocean Geotron* (1966), but by the 1960s he was pushing at an open door. Pulp SF was the dominant genre of mid-century America. But in 1910 Tom's adventures were ground-breaking. In *Tom Swift and His Submarine Boat*, Tom and his inventor father create a prototype submarine called the *Advance*, and with a small crew set off to the coast of Uruguay to recover gold bullion from a sunken ship, pursued by an unscrupulous group of scavengers in another submarine.

The very public launch in 1954 of the first nuclear-powered submarine in the world, USS *Nautilus*, gave a whole new impetus to comic and pop-cultural depictions of super-advanced submarines. In the mid-1950s the American Comics Group's short-lived but now cult comic-book series *Commander Battle and the Atomic Sub* predicted that by 1962 the 'atomic submarine' would have caterpillar treads and wheels for land deployment and would even be able to rocket-boost itself into space. Commander Battle's submarine was actually a sophisticated mini-submarine with a four-man crew, the 'atomic commandoes', who fought UFOs and alien invaders as well as the Red Menace.

British children also had fun with submarines, if with less technical verisimilitude than was provided by the Tom Swift stories for American children. The long-running *Iron Fish* series (1951–67) in the popular children's comic *The Beano* followed the adventures of Danny and Penny Gray and the incredible submersible vessels built for them by

World Aquanaut Security Patrol (WASP) submarine *Stingray* in the TV series of the same name (1964).

their inventor father, Professor Gray, which were equipped with extreme manoeuvrability and a sharp-tipped nose for attacking enemies.

Alan Moore incorporated the *Iron Fish* back story into *The League of Extraordinary Gentlemen* when a young boy, Jimmy Grey, is rescued from the Thames by Nemo and the *Nautilus* after Martian Tripods destroy a packed train crossing the river, killing all the passengers, including his parents. 'Your metal fish is very grand, sir,' he tells Nemo after being put ashore. 'God willing, I shall build one myself.'[5] In supplementary material about past and future Leagues, we learn that Jimmy Grey grew up to become Professor James Grey, designer of 'an impressive sword-fish style submarine', an exact replica of the submersibles of *The Iron Fish*, and joined the short-lived post-Second World War version of the League.

Moore continued to play with Nemo and *Nautilus* throughout the marginalia of the League stories. The multi-genre meta-story *League of Extraordinary Gentlemen: Black Dossier* contains a two-page diagrammatic cross-section of the *Nautilus*, with the initial 1865 design taken from Verne's novel added to in 1878 by a new 'Kraken section' attached to the original 'whale hull', the new section containing additional firepower, a retractable cannon and mechanical tentacles to make it more formidable. One of the more playful additions was a mock-comic game, 'How to Make Nemo's *Nautilus*', complete with illustrations to assist children to make a paper version:

> 'Oh please, Captain Nemo,' gasped Simon and Sally. 'Please take us for a ride in your wonderful Nautilus!' 'Why, I can't do that, you mewling whelps of the hated British Empire', replies the Sikh submariner agreeably, 'but I can show you how to make your own!'[6]

Part of the charm of the eponymous submarine in Gerry Anderson's *Stingray* (1964–5), filmed in 'Supermarionation' with Anderson's puppets as the characters, was that it looked as if it *had* been constructed by children. The physical constraints of Anderson's puppets, particularly their inability to walk convincingly, meant that he developed situations and vessels such as the Thunderbirds and *Stingray* where they had, out of necessity, to be seated much of the time.

The *Stingray* was a small, high-speed combat submarine of the World Aquanaut Security Patrol (WASP) of 2060 that could reach a speed of 600 knots and descend to 36,000 ft. In the opening episode *Stingray* discovers the underwater civilization of Titanica ruled by ruthless King Triton and his warrior elite the Aquaphibians. Only the rebellion of the mute slave girl Marina allows it to escape and warn WASP of the threat beneath the waves. *Stingray* was captained by lantern-jawed Troy Tempest, supported by his cheerful working-class subordinate 'Phones' (for Hydrophones). Although the submarine's adventures extended to encounters with strange creatures and natural disasters, most of the show focused on the threat from the Aquaphibians, aided covertly by their 'enemy within', Agent X-20, a saboteur placed within WASP by the exotic Triton. *Stingray* was energetic and poppy fun ('Anything can happen in the next half hour!') but its place in the early 1960s Cold War era is clearly established.

The 1960s were a brief and unique period of hyper-accelerated cultural change. Just a few years after *Stingray*'s launch a very different type of submarine with a very different type of crew was offered in *Yellow Submarine* (dir. George Dunning, 1968). With the passage of time this has assumed, along with Verne's *Nautilus*, the status of *the* fictional submarine of popular culture. But whereas the Beatles' song of the same name, released in 1966, was simple nonsense verse written to suit Ringo Starr's limited vocal range, the film fuses the style and imagery of Pop art, Aubrey Beardsley and Japanese anime into a singular artistic vision.

The story of the magical island paradise of Pepperland and its invasion by the music-hating Blue Meanies was literally made for the Beatles. Directed by the animator George Dunning, its screenplay benefited from uncredited dialogue by the poet Roger McGough. Although the Beatles were initially indifferent to the film (which was made to fulfil a contractual obligation), once they saw what was being produced and how it gelled perfectly with their own marriage of northern whimsy and psychedelic utopianism, they became more enthusiastic.

The Blue Meanies, who drain Pepperland of all colour and music before a lone native, Old Fred, takes the Yellow Submarine to Liverpool to seek help, clearly represent negativity and soullessness. The multiple doorways and landscapes – the Sea of Time, the Sea of Holes, the Sea of Nothing – that the Yellow Submarine must traverse all challenge conventional notions of linearity and logic.

Connecting them all is the Yellow Submarine itself, a narrative device that has received surprisingly little attention on its own account. Yet the hijacking of the traditional grey-black colour scheme used for submarines by one of the brightest and least military of the primary colours could hardly be more apparent. Yellow is eternally transgressive, the preferred colour of late nineteenth-century aesthetes and poets; the cover and title of the infamous *Yellow Book* illustrated by Aubrey Beardsley was a direct influence on the animation style of the film.

In a roundtable academic discussion in 2003 hosted by the American radical poet Joan Houlihan, her fellow poet Joe Amato explicitly identified the iconography of the Yellow Submarine with the general philosophy of avant-garde art, at least in the crucial period of the 1960s, and suggested that the terms were interchangeable. Of the 1960s he said:

> At least in retrospect, the term 'yellow submarine' captures the stylized innocence of that camp-saturated era, arguably the last great era of widespread social change, when a collective apprehension of, an attitude about, belief in a fiction of the possible, as opposed to merely the probable, became part and parcel of everyday life. During the sixties, the yellow submarine was a prime embodiment of such fictive leaning . . . So the yellow submarine is, in a fundamental sense, forever. It reclaims the public domain as a domain of freethinking public action – it brings all citizens in from the cold ambience of social neglect

and injustice – and it torpedoes power brokers where they live by insisting that their love of power is but a corrupted application of the power of love. The yellow submarine makes power brokers look silly, and therein lies its transformational power.[7]

As Amato instinctively understood, the *yellowness* of the Yellow Submarine is its point, a permanent rebuke to those who would never dream of turning a submarine into a psychedelic dream-machine or singing 'All You Need Is Love'. Like *Alice's Adventures in Wonderland*, *Monty Python* and *The Goodies*, it captures the surreal and anarchistic strain running through British culture. Such is its enduring appeal that a large, floating yellow submarine balloon was used in Danny Boyle's 2012 London Olympics opening ceremony, one icon enfolding another in a seamless self-referential loop.

Alan Moore would have appreciated the dialectic. In *The New Traveller's Almanac* – a seemingly whimsical but actually essential annex to the main narrative of *The League of Extraordinary Gentlemen* – he provides a forty-page cartography of the entirety of imaginative fiction in which various narrators from the League's extended history (Orlando, Gulliver, Mina Murray, Nemo) draw together every manifestation of myth, legend, folk tale, hidden land, lost world and wondrous realm to compile a comprehensive, alternative *Rough Guide* to all of Earth's continents and oceans.

In the section covering 'The Americas', Captain Nemo's log books for 1897 record that after passing Tierra del Fuego,

> The locals tell tales of an English naval Sergeant, one James Winston Pepper, lost at sea in 1870, supposedly dragged down through undertows through emerald waters and eventually washed up upon the shores of a subsurface paradise where harmony reigned everywhere. The realm, named Pepper's Land, is reputably the source of the garishly coloured phantom submarine we've sighted.[8]

In his final *League* series, *Tempest*, which takes us to the near-future, Moore delves deeper into the fate of Pepperland. In the first issue the remains of the League – Mina, Orlando and Emma Peel, pursued by spymaster and serial rapist James Bond – journey to the South Atlantic and discover what is left of the island, which 'took a lot of damage during the Falklands War'. As they pass Pepperland they see the shattered remains of the Yellow Submarine on the shore, surrounded by skeletons and debris, a sad reminder of more optimistic times.[9]

Throughout *Tempest* Moore deconstructs and reinvents the motif of the fantasy submarine, invoking both *Nautilus* and *Stingray*. The headline of Issue 2's mock newspaper cover is 'Dugong Missing!' (a dugong being a small marine mammal) with the subheading 'Iconic Sub Feared Lost'. A sub-heading tells us: 'SPECTRUM to deploy nuclear sub in Arctic Circle', a reference to the text, in which Bond orders an SSBN to fire a nuclear missile into the Blazing World, the hidden Arctic sanctuary of the founder and protector of the League, Shakespeare's Duke Prospero, and the home of Imagination. By this action a specific idea of the submarine destroys the Idea Space from which it emerged.

Unabashedly impractical versions of the submarine/submersible are utilized in a variety of contexts, the most unlikely of which is the mini-submarine *Proteus* of the cult SF film *Fantastic Voyage* (1966). The *Proteus*, crewed by a four-person team from the Combined Miniature Deterrent Force, is shrunk to the size of a molecule and injected into the bloodstream of a spy who holds crucial information obtained from the Soviets, although it can only stay miniaturized for one hour before reverting to full size. Unique and striking effects enhance the sense of discovery integral to the early SF of Verne and Wells, as the submarine navigates through deadly obstacles such as blood clots and white blood cells.

The *Proteus* is in a literal line of inheritance from Verne's *Nautilus*. The director of *Fantastic Voyage*, Richard Fleischer, also directed the classic 1954 Disney adaptation of *20,000 Leagues Under the Sea*. For *Fantastic Voyage* he specifically requested that the art director and designer of Disney's *Nautilus*, Harper Goff, create the equally iconic *Proteus*. As a result of Goff's inventive design, and the animated series of *Fantastic Voyage* that ran from 1968 to 1970 and thereafter in syndication, the *Proteus* now sits with the *Nautilus* and *Stingray* in enduring popular affection.

The *Proteus* shared a complete lack of scientific credibility with *Skydiver One*, the hybrid submarine-jet fighter of Gerry Anderson's TV series *UFO* (1970), in which the secret global organization SHADOW defends Earth from covert attack by hostile alien craft. SHADOW deploys Interceptors in space and a range of defence weapons on Earth, most notably *Skydiver One*, a super-advanced submarine whose bow section is a twin-engined Interceptor, *Sky 1*, which can be launched underwater and take the fight to Earth's skies. *Skydiver One* is showcased in UFO's stylish opening credits (one of the slickest and sexiest products of early 1970s chic) as it angles to 45 degrees and fires *Sky 1* out of the ocean into the atmosphere.

Anderson was a genius at designing and presenting vessels that would capture a child's imagination for life. In the classic children's series *Thunderbirds* he gave British children the most beloved and instantly recognizable submersible in popular fiction, the small but hardy *Thunderbird 4*, hatched from the much larger *Thunderbird 2* but still essential to many underwater rescues. *Thunderbird 4* was bright yellow, two years before the song and four years before the film that appropriated the colour for its own iconic submarine.

The *Proteus*, *Skydiver* and *Thunderbird 4*, along with similar outrageous vessels such as the Penguin's customized submarine in the 1966 *Batman* film, are Pop Art versions of the 'fantasy submarine', a friendly and unthreatening vision that passed comparatively quickly, to be replaced by the more enduring steampunk submarine. Steampunk as a genre attained self-identity in April 1987 when, in a letter to the SF literary journal *Locus*, the SF author K. W. Jeter coined the phrase to describe the mixture of alternate history and retro-technology that he and like-minded friends were producing at the time. Although steampunk as a literary form had clear antecedents (particularly Michael Moorcock's *A Nomad of the Time Streams* trilogy of the adventures of Captain Oswald Bastable), Jeter's *Morlock Night* (1979) has a good claim to be its first conscious product.

Morlock Night begins after the events described in *The Time Machine*, when the time traveller returns to the year 802,701 and is killed by the Morlocks. Intelligent Morlock generals then use his machine to travel back to 1895 to build a Morlock army in London's sewers. After various narrative twists the story ventures underneath London to the Lost Coin World, a subterranean world where the homeless misfits of London scrape a living. This is revealed as an offshoot of a long-destroyed Atlantean civilization, one of whose relics, a clockwork submarine lifted straight from Verne, has been stolen by the Morlocks. The submarine is the centre of a tense set piece when it becomes clear that neither Morlocks nor humans can operate it, and it crash dives in the vast underground lake beneath London.[10]

Morlock Night, for all its entertainment value, is no *20,000 Leagues*. It is a preliminary sketch of what would later become the fully realized concept of a steampunk submarine. Jules Verne's original *Nautilus*, for example, is not and cannot be steampunk, although Walt Disney's certainly is. At the time the book was published in 1870, Verne's submarine was at the cutting edge of its era's speculative thought, the AI of its day. Its technology is fresh and contemporary, not retro-futuristic.

The central element of the steampunk submarine that Verne bequeathed to later literary culture was an obsession with the nuts and bolts of the vessel, with pumps and airtanks, steel and chrome, charts and maps and leather armchairs. This took a century of cultural osmosis to fully take hold. Even though the first steampunk novels saw print in the 1970s it was not until the 1990s that its design aesthetic expanded into a distinct subculture in literature, technology and fashion.

The hypothetical use of a more technologically advanced submarine in the era of the American Civil War has been a source of fascination to more than one writer. Cherie Priest's 'Clockwork Century' series of steampunk novels (2009–16) has offered one of the more intriguing extrapolations. A politically subversive, blue-collar version of conventional urban steampunk – whose protagonists tend to be rebellious aristocrats or alternate versions of unorthodox scientists such as Ada Byron or Nikola Tesla – the Clockwork Century's heroes are miners, soldiers, pirates, scavengers, con artists and prostitutes.

The first novel in the series, *Boneshaker* (2009), was nominated for both the Hugo and Nebula awards. The series begins in the remote northwest city of Seattle in 1862 when a mining disaster releases 'blight gas' that turns those breathing it into the living dead, or 'rotters', and then expands to encompass a civil war that has ground on for twenty years through deployment of classic steampunk technology – dirigible airships, automated 'walkers' and juggernaut trains. The third novel in the series, *Ganymede* (2011), has New Orleans threatened by the occupying forces of Texas, an independent state in uneasy alliance with the Confederacy against the Union, and a growing army of rotters who roam the bayous.

Ganymede centres on Josephine Early, a mixed-race New Orleans brothel-keeper who is also part of a Black underground resistance to Texan and Confederate power. To this end she hires airship pirate Captain Adnan Cly to steer a sunken submarine, the advanced prototype *Ganymede*, out of the Mississippi to the Gulf of Mexico, and there deliver it to the U.S. Navy. In Priest's timeline the *Ganymede* is created to replace the lost *Hunley* and to break the North's naval blockade. It is the missing link, technologically and chronologically, between the *Hunley* and Verne's *Nautilus*, and is crucial to the outcome of the long Civil War. In a tense climax the submarine escapes on to the Gulf, where it wreaks havoc on Texan surface ships before being handed over to the North. History, already rewritten, is rewritten again.

Having established the template for the steampunk submarine in its 1954 adaptation of *20,000 Leagues*, Disney returned to it in *Atlantis: The Lost Empire* (2001), an animated adventure about an early twentieth-century expedition to find the fabled city. In its initial stages the

expedition is conducted on the exploratory submarine *Ulysses*, a gigantic version of the *Nautilus*, clearly influenced by Harper Goff's 1954
designs. Launched by being dropped from a crane into the water, the
Ulysses drives and dominates the first half of the narrative. When the
submarine is damaged, forcing the crew to abandon it, *Atlantis* loses
its focus.

    Atlantis demonstrated that Disney had little more to add to the
fantasy submarine. In any event that torch had been taken up by others,
most particularly the Czech animated fantasy film-maker Karel Zeman
in his masterpiece *Invention for Destruction* (1958), which won the 1958
International Film Festival's Grand Prix award for its visual audacity.
Based on Verne's *Facing the Flag*, Zeman's delightful and astonishing
film is a thematic more than a literal adaptation, a loving homage
saturated with the wonder and imagination of Verne's entire corpus.

    The production design of Zeman's work, most especially *Invention
for Destruction*, simulated the original nineteenth-century illustrations
of Verne's novels by Riou and de Neuville. A collage of multi-layered
animation techniques, such as woodprints, matte painting, puppetry

*Invention for
Destruction* (1958,
dir. Karel Zeman).

and models, seamlessly integrated with cut-out and stop-motion shots, produce a vision as unique and memorable as that of his American counterpart, Ray Harryhausen. Stock footage of sea and sky is repainted and fused into the animation. Like *Monty Python* meets *Yellow Submarine*, but with more texture and depth, Zeman's is an unclassifiable visual style ludicrously labelled 'Mysti-Mation' for the dubbed American version, *The Fabulous World of Jules Verne*.

Zeman developed an aesthetic for Verne's creations as memorable as even Disney's. But while loyal to Verne's style and period, Zeman followed Disney in one important respect. He too updated Verne to imply that the narrative's submarine (both the *Nautilus* and Roch's invention) was powered by some form of proto-nuclear reactor, or, as *Invention for Destruction* had it, 'the secret of matter'. He also replaced *Facing the Flag*'s climactic submarine battle with a submarine chasing a (rather quaint) wooden rescue submersible.

Zeman's fantastical visions shared a visual style and energy with Japanese manga and anime, a tradition itself traceable to Wells and Verne. In the early twentieth century the Japanese SF writer Shunro

Invention for Destruction (1958, dir. Karel Zeman).

Oshikawa created a Japanese version of Captain Nemo and the *Nautilus*. Oshikawa's *The Undersea Warship* (1903) and its five sequels established a fictional universe for Japan as powerful and enduring as that of Sherlock Holmes for the Anglo-American world.

Oshikawa's novels follow the adventures of Captain Sakuragi and his 'undersea battleship' the *Denko tei*, which fights for Japan on, under and occasionally even above the waves. Unlike Nemo, Captain Sakuragi is a fervent nationalist whose motivation for developing the *Denko tei* is exasperation with the failure of Japan's civilian government to resist the expansion of Western powers in Asia. After the Russo-Japanese War of 1904–5, the course of which Oshikawa had predicted, his work became extremely popular in Japan and influenced both Japanese SF and the rise of militarist fascism in Japanese society in the 1930s.

The film adaptations of Oshikawa's work were very loose. The most successful, *Atragon* (1963), based in part on *The Undersea Warship*, updated the story from the early twentieth century to the 1960s and replaced the historically credible threat of Western imperialist armies with the rather less credible Lost Continent of Mu. Like the predicted atomic sub of American popular comics, *Atragon*'s advanced submarine was fitted with flight capability and a massive drill that enabled it to burrow through landmass.

Other fantasy submarine films, such as those of the U.S.–Japanese co-production *Latitude Zero* (1969), remain cinematic curios. Directed by Ishiro Honda from a script by the American SF writer Ted Sherdeman *Latitude Zero* centres on an improbable two-hundred-year-old war between the super-submarines *Alpha* and *Black Shark*, battling over the undersea kingdom of the title, a paradise with unexplained age-defying properties. The *Alpha*'s commander (Joseph Cotton) is a Nemo-like figure and *Latitude Zero* has elements of Vernian wonder, but the film is undone by a profusion of poorly imagined mutant monsters.

Latitude Zero was an attempt to realize on screen early manga such as *Blue Submarine No. 6* (1967), a simple tale of the far future where the evil scientist Zorndyke has caused the mass flooding of human cities. Only mankind's submarines, especially No. 6, can defeat him and his hybrid creatures. Following the international success of the 1988 film *Akira* (based upon Katsuhiro Otomo's manga of 1982–90, a series as influential as *Blade Runner* and *Neuromancer* in creating the core elements of the cyberpunk genre), the medium developed in scope and maturity, and its fantasy submarines were revisioned.

The hugely successful manga series *Arpeggio of Blue Steel* (2009–present) and its anime adaptation (2013) begins in the year 2039, after rising sea levels have eroded the world's coastlines, this time the result of climate change rather than a villain's machinations. At this point a mysterious fleet of AI-controlled sentient warships labelled the 'Fleet of Fog' appear from nowhere, defeat all military opposition and establish a series of aerial and naval blockades which divide the world's nations from each other.

In *Arpeggio of Blue Steel* the submarine is both threat and saviour. The threat is technological. The saviour is the ghost in the machine, in this case the capacity of the Fleet's humanoid avatars to develop self-awareness and independent thought. *Arpeggio* follows one of these 'Mental Models', the embodied consciousness of submarine *I-401*, which has taken the form of a young girl called Iona and defected from the Fleet to help the humans.[11]

Despite a hard SF aesthetic, *Arpeggio of Blue Steel* and similar manga such as *Dream Hunter Rem* and *Attack on Titan* often contain elements of the mystical and supernatural (or, at least, the non-rationally explicable), seldom fully integrated with the narrative. But the disjunction *is* the point. The intrusion of the supernatural into the submarine genre – ostensibly the most scientific and mechanistic of narrative formats – produces its own affect. The submarine, or at least a submarine lost, sunk, displaced, partakes of the cultural theorist Mark Fisher's concept of the eerie – the not right, out of place, out of *this* place – a sense that Adam Roberts exploits skilfully in *Twenty Trillion Leagues*.

One does not have to look far for real-world analogues. On the morning of 4 March 1970 all contact with the French diesel-electric submarine *Eurydice*, diving in calm seas off Cape Camerat near St Tropez, was suddenly lost. A month later, after an extensive search operation, shattered pieces of the *Eurydice* were found on the seabed off St Tropez. A large fragment of the submarine's stern was resting in the centre of a strange, anomalous crater 30 metres in diameter. All fragments of the submarine were oddly twisted and deformed.

The submarine as a repository of the eerie has been successfully exploited in film and literature, most particularly in David Twohy's underrated *Below* (2002). Written by Darren Aronofsky, whose directorial efforts *Pi*, *Noah* and *Mother!* are all exercises in extreme sensibility, *Below* is a taut and effective supernatural chiller. The tale of USS *Tiger Shark*, a Second World War American submarine with a dark secret, filters a classic ghost story through tight, dripping interiors, successfully peeling back the crew's military discipline through the creeping realization that the ghost of the submarine's murdered captain is still with them, seeking revenge.

Below stays within genre boundaries, if conjoined ones. *Snowpiercer* (2013), an English-language South Korean–Czech co-production directed by Bong Joon-ho, is absolutely *sui generis*. Based on the French graphic novel *Le Transperceneige* (1982), *Snowpiercer* is set after an attempt to avert global warming by altering the world's weather patterns catastrophically backfires and plunges Earth into a new Ice Age. The only survivors reside on a 1,001 carriage super-train called the *Snowpiercer* which endlessly circumnavigates the globe.

The train is a mini-society of its own with sharply drawn class distinctions. The sumptuous front sections are inhabited by a privileged elite, the mid-sections are a buffer zone of engineering and hydroponics with sleeping dorms and cafeterias, and the rear sections hold the proletarian serfs, kept in cattle-truck conditions and fed gelatinous food bars by the train's shock troops.

The film's central conceit of a total vacuum-sealed class divide thus exploits the visual extremes of the submarine in popular fiction. The *Snowpiercer*'s design aesthetic is a gigantic fusion of the diesel-electric submarine with plush, romantic steampunk. The train's working-class rear sections are a grungy and claustrophobic U-boat, while the ruling-class forward sections, with luxurious salons, swimming pool and library, are extravagant aspects of Prince Dakkar's *Nautilus*. The *Snowpiercer* is ripe for revolution.

Joon-ho's astonishing film erases genre identity as easily as its eponymous vehicle cuts through pack ice. In the same manner that Cherie Priest's 'Clockwork Century' proved that steampunk submarines need not function as part of an alternate British Empire or a Japanese post-apocalyptic AI, *Snowpiercer* demonstrates that the submarine genre need not include a submarine at all.

ENLIST IN THE WAVES

RELEASE A MAN TO FIGHT AT SEA

Apply to your nearest
NAVY RECRUITING STATION OR OFFICE OF NAVAL OFFICER PROCUREMENT

6

THE SUBMARINE AND SEX

Equality came late to the submarine service. In America the dam began to crack with the creation in 1942 of the United States Naval Reserve (Women's Reserve), better known as WAVES (Women Accepted for Volunteer Emergency Service). After Pearl Harbor efforts were made to create a women's reserve force in which women would hold naval ranks but the Department of the Navy opposed the idea. It took the personal intervention of Eleanor Roosevelt to shift this opposition and to secure the support of her husband for a women's reserve, resulting in the passing of Public Law 689 in July 1942 formally establishing the WAVES.

The programme was designed to free up men on the home front for service overseas, leaving many positions previously held only by men – in medicine, intelligence, cryptography, cartography, communications, logistics and engineering – to be taken by women. Although they held enlisted and officer ranks, WAVES were not allowed to serve on board naval vessels and were without command authority except within the Women's Reserve. Many encountered hostility from male colleagues. Secretary of the Navy Frank Knox, a virulent racist, made clear that African American WAVES would be recruited 'over my dead body'.[1] This was literally the case. Only after he died in 1944 were several African American women allowed to serve.

The WAVES were wound up in 1946 yet their example sowed the seed for later advances in diversity and equality across U.S. naval forces, advances that the submarine service was the last to incorporate. Although women have served on U.S. Navy surface ships since 1993, it was not until 2011 that they were permitted to serve on submarines, when the first 24 female officers reported for duty on four submarines.

One of the main reasons for not allowing this earlier was, as a 1995 report by the Chief of Naval Operations explained, 'whether the added complications of a mixed-gender crew will undermine the operational effectiveness of the ship'.[2] Among these 'added complications' were, at least ostensibly, the need to ensure privacy in the use of bathroom facilities, and therefore the installation of new on-board toilets, and concerns about the possible effect of background radiation on pregnant women.

Despite these problems a Senate Advisory Committee on the issue continued to press for the necessary redesigns of submarines that would assist the process of gender integration. These efforts finally bore fruit when, in January 2010, President Obama's Secretary of Defense

Chief information systems technician Jessica Cooper oversees operations on the guided-missile submarine USS *Ohio* (SSGN 726), January 2021.

informed Congress that, regardless of objections and obstacles, this was the policy and it would now be implemented.

Some other countries did better. In 1985 the Norwegian Navy became the first in the world to permit women to serve in submarines, followed by the Danish Navy in 1988, the Swedish Navy in 1989, the Australian Navy in 1998, the Spanish Navy in 1999, the German Navy in 2001 and the Canadian Navy in 2002. The UK changed its 'no women on submarines' policy in 2011 and in May 2014 the first three female submariners – Lieutenants Alexandra Olsson, Maxine Stiles and Penny Thackray – took up their posts in the service. In September 2014 medic and nuclear physicist Emma Boswell became the first 'out' lesbian to serve on a submarine.

There is a dark side to this progressive history. The first female to serve on board an Argentine submarine, Lieutenant Eliana Krawczyk, was also the first to die on one. In November 2017 the Argentine diesel-electric submarine ARA *San Juan* disappeared off the east coast of Argentina while on a routine training exercise, with the loss of its 43-person crew. The wreck of the *San Juan* was only discovered a year later, broken into several pieces on the ocean floor.

The marginalization of female characters from the fictional submarine genre mirrors the general history of the last seventy years. To the extent that integration is an extremely recent development this is an accurate, though uncritical, reflection of real-world sexism. While Reeman and Fullerton's naval fictions, to say nothing of the wider range of classic submarine Boys Own adventures, were products of their time, the most visible marginalization of women inside the genre has been in the most visual medium: cinema.

This was obvious even to itself. 'What's the matter, Burke?' asks one of the trapped submariners of his taciturn comrade in John Ford's *Men Without Women*. 'Is the subject of women taboo in this sardine can?' Well might he ask. The 'subject of women' is an elephant in the room within the submarine genre whose loud absence, or silent presence, hangs over many of its narratives.

Although there has always been a popular cinema aimed explicitly at women audiences, from Douglas Sirk's 1950s melodramas to Jane Campion's deconstructions of female desire in the 1990s, these are notable exceptions to a broad rule. Until relatively recently the male gaze in cinema was omnipresent, comprising that of the male director and editor, the male characters within the film's fictional world, and the audience receiving the image. It did not matter if half the audience were female. Their subjectivity was (and in most mainstream film still is) irrelevant. If it cannot, as in the submarine genre, construct and manipulate a literal female image for male pleasure, then it will find an acceptable libidinal substitute in which to invest desire. Military technology, particularly weaponry, is often that substitute.

The code phrase used by the u.s. submarine service to confirm that a successfully launched torpedo is on target and trajectory – 'Hot, Straight and Normal' – is unimprovable as an unwitting expression of the genre's aggressive male heterosexuality. In *Crimson Tide* the analogy of the torpedo or ballistic missile with penetrative sex is made explicit when, speaking of rogue Russian nationalists possibly about to arm nuclear missiles, one of the petty officers who support the conservative captain against the liberal xo declares, 'You don't put on a condom if you're not gonna fuck.'

Tom Clancy, with a Midwestern lack of self-awareness, first channelled this subterranean sexuality in the techno-thriller. His descriptions of military tech were imbued with genuine ecstasy, each individual weapon or weapon system lovingly named, analysed and catalogued for later deployment in the narrative, teased and held back until finally reaching climactic release as Jack Ryan and the White House brought the hammer down on America's foreign enemies.

Clancy's heir apparent, Patrick Robinson, pulled the same trick, but with added subliminal arousal. Robinson made quite explicit that the focus of his and his male protagonists' obsession and passion is not a woman, or indeed a man, but the submarine itself:

Commander Dunning's boat was one of the first of the Los
Angeles-Class to be fitted with the new WLY-I acoustic intercept
and countermeasures system. State-of-the-art EHF communications were already in place. Special acoustic tile-cladding,
designed to reduce her active-sonar target signature, made her
one of the stealthiest submarines ever built . . . She was twice as
fast as a Kilo, twice as big, and twice as lethal.[3]

After Tony Scott's enormously popular *Top Gun* had glamorized
U.S. fighter jets as balletic sex toys of the skies, Scott transferred its
vibratory aesthetic to *Crimson Tide*. His film includes several long, lin-
gering shots of the SSBN *Alabama* effortlessly penetrating the sea, rising
from the depths or plunging to the deep to the accompaniment of a
rousing score. That the film's throbbing techno-sexual vibe has more
in common with David Cronenberg's *Crash* than the careful liberal
values of its script is just one reason *Crimson Tide* is such a problematic
and contradictory narrative.

The sexualization of military kit, weaponry and vessels in the
modern submarine thriller runs from outright Ballardian fetishism to
parodies of heterosexual marriage, and flows directly from naval tradition. Vessels of the Anglo-American naval services are all known by
the female signifier. To its overwhelmingly male crew a ship, boat or
submarine is 'she', and as such is frequently the object of sentimental
regard and veneration. Not for nothing does the captain perish with
the ship. It is the duty of the husband to remain with his partner until
death do them part.

In the absence of women, the social collective on the submarine
unconsciously adopt traditional gender roles, specifically the captain
as 'father' and the XO as 'mother'. This is not a forced analogy. The roles
are built into the command structure and responsibilities of submarine
forces. It is the XO's job to be alert to the emotional balance of the crew
and to intercede for them with the more distant captain who, burdened
by command and strategic decisions, does not have time for such things.

This dichotomy is often dramatized in fictional representation, such as in *Crimson Tide*, *K19* and *Run Silent, Run Deep*.

In comparison to Alistair MacLean's early 1960s Cold War thriller, Michael Crichton's *Sphere* concedes not only that women have a valid place in underwater exploration, but that they would be far better suited to it than men. When asked why all the support staff in the underwater habitat are women, the expedition's military leader, Captain Barnes, answers that 'women are far superior for submerged operations' because they are physically smaller, consume less nutrients and air, and have better social skills in confined spaces. 'The fact is,' he admits, 'the navy long ago recognised that all their submariners should be female. But just try to implement that one.'[4]

Most (I think probably all) submarine films completely fail the Bechdel Test: does the film contain at least one scene where two women talk to each other about something other than a man? Failure to pass the test does not automatically discredit a film if the test could never have been met due to the nature of the narrative (for example, Peter Weir's superb *Master and Commander* (2003), a close cousin of the submarine film set entirely on board a British naval frigate during the Napoleonic Wars), and if the film concerned does not further privilege the male through uncritical representation of a stereotypical heroic ideal.

Most submarine films fail this test as well. In the film of *Voyage to the Bottom of the Sea* there are only two female characters. One is Admiral Nelson's secretary, who although performing only secretarial duties holds the rank of lieutenant. Despite this, she is introduced with a shot of her shapely rear jigging back and forth to the beat of Frankie Avalon's trumpet. She is engaged to the *Seaview*'s captain and is literally counting the days, hours and minutes until their wedding. The other female character is a navy psychologist (Joan Fontaine). Ostensibly the film's co-lead, at the end she is revealed as a saboteur and is casually tossed to the killer shark kept in the *Seaview*'s large aquarium.

The TV series of *Voyage to the Bottom of the Sea* hit an incredible low for female representation, even for its time. While *Star Trek* featured a Black female officer, Lieutenant Uhura, among the main cast, the fourth series of *Voyage*, broadcast at the same time (1968), had no female roles at all in any of its 25 episodes, not even non-speaking ones. No one involved in its production, and few of its audience, would have even noticed this.

The submarine genre, even more than the traditional war film – which sometimes includes female characters as nurses, technicians, resistance fighters or civilians – was and is known for gender exclusivity. Sometimes the narrative could do little else, for example in productions such as *Destination Tokyo*, *We Dive at Dawn* and *Das Boot*. Sometimes, by virtue of a peacetime setting or a plot that incorporated land-based action, it was possible to include female characters.

Men Without Women, despite its title, is not without women. It was made in 1929, in a brief, liberating period between the first use of sound in film and the introduction of the self-censoring, puritanical Hays Code of 1934. For four to five years American sound films could and did experiment with sexual themes, language and imagery, to an extent and with a freedom not seen again until the 1960s.

Thus the initial scenes of *Men Without Women* take place in Shanghai in what is clearly a brothel. When the submarine captain good-naturedly sets up a virginal sailor with a prostitute, his crewmates all approve, and there is no indication that this is behaviour the audience is expected to frown on. Later, the drunken crew stroll past sex workers in display windows. One is even in a cage. The crew find this amusing, stopping to sing to her.

By contrast, *Destination Tokyo* makes an explicit point about the moral superiority of a stable marriage over loose sexual behaviour. After the death of the popular father-figure Mike, the crew find among his possessions a 'Record-a-voice' vinyl record from his wife and play it, gathering together to listen to a touching encomium to their happy marriage and family life. As the submariners listen they grow somber and drift away, all except the inveterate womanizer Wolf, who stays to the end and absorbs the message of a good woman.

Driving this point home, the film asserts that the American family unit, built on heterosexual marriage, is morally superior to its Japanese equivalent, because it is more firmly grounded in male love for the female. In a scene in which the submarine's senior officers discuss Japanese culture, the captain explains that Japanese families routinely sell their young daughters to factories, 'or worse', because in Japan, 'Females are useful there only to work or to have children. The Japs don't understand the love we have for our women. They don't even have a word for it in their language.'

Quintessentially male film genres often employ the standard Madonna-whore dichotomy in representing women, a trope alive and kicking today (for a recent example, see the deeply hip and cine-literate *Baby Driver* of 2017). In the submarine/naval adventure this division is usually between the 'good-time girl' in a foreign port and the angelic sweetheart or wife at home, who is idealized in her absence. In *Run Silent, Run Deep* the crew have a 1940s-era erotic pin-up in the ratings' mess which all the men superstitiously pat for good luck every time battle stations is called, a fusion of sex object and religious icon, Madonna *and* whore.

The vintage submarine comedy *Operation Petticoat* (1959) is the *ne plus ultra* of the representation of women in the submarine genre. On the surface an amiable comedy containing nothing so unpleasant as sexual assault, rape or harassment, *Operation Petticoat* exudes good nature and its light comedy beats are delivered flawlessly by Cary Grant and Tony Curtis. This does not prevent the film being one long wallow in the male gaze, a two-hour meta-assault on the generic female. The life of the U.S. submarine *Tiger Shark,* already on its last legs owing to a surprise Japanese attack a few weeks after Pearl Harbor, is turned upside down when it is forced to take on board five stranded U.S. Navy nurses including Lieutenant Duran (Dina Merrill) and the ditzy, Marilyn Monroe-like Lieutenant Crandell (Joan O'Brien). The presence of the nurses disturbs and disrupts the life of the boat, with most of the crew responding like hormonal adolescents. No sooner are the

Poster for *Operation Petticoat* (dir. Blake Edwards, 1959).

women on board than the men begin smartening up, wearing cologne and faking illness to get attention.

The submarine's predicament is symbolized by its needing to effect repairs in the Philippines, where the only primer paint colours it can secure, red and white, result in an entirely pink hull. Although this has nothing to do with the nurses, the transformation of the submarine from steely grey to feminine pink (in the conventional social construction of gender, the stereotypical colour of and for girls) is presented as the inevitable result of the *Sea Tiger* taking women on board. Where else could such an action end but in public emasculation?

'If anybody ever asks you what you're fighting for, there's your answer,' says the grizzled Chief of the Boat to a young sailor when they first see the nurses. Thereafter, the assumption that the women are the men's rightful possession, a prize to be collected, the object of a hunt in which the women themselves have no say, is relentless. 'When a girl's under 21 she's protected by law. When she's over 65 she's protected by nature. Anywhere in between, she's fair game,' says Sherman, who can hardly complain when Holden organizes a raffle for the nurses among the crew only a few minutes after their arrival.

The women, although identified as WAVES officers, are slighted throughout, by the male characters and the script itself. No sooner are they on board than Crandell accidentally hits the collision alarm. Shortly after this she accidentally launches a torpedo. The climactic joke of the film, safely assuming a collective laugh from a male audience and their painfully complicit wives and girlfriends, comes when the *Sea Tiger* must convince a pursuing U.S. destroyer that it is an American vessel and not a Japanese submarine in disguise. To do so, Sherman orders that it jettison the women's lingerie. Upon seeing Crandell's generous bra floating on the sea through his binoculars, the captain of the destroyer ceases bombardment, on the grounds that 'The Japanese have nothing like this.'

From the tagline on its poster – 'Submerged with 5 girls . . . no wonder the SS *Sea Tiger* turned a shocking pink!'– to its sentimental coda, *Operation Petticoat* is a barrage of jocular sexism that cannot be excused as merely symptomatic of its era. Other mainstream films of the time with major comedic elements such as *The King and I* (1956) and *Indiscreet* (1958) portrayed female characters with dignity and agency, yet *Operation Petticoat* sees women as nothing but a silly, vexing distraction, sexual objects for peacetime enjoyment that have unreasonably trespassed on male territory. Their proper roles are re-established at the close, set years later, when it is established that Captain Sherman (Grant) and Lieutenant Holden (Curtis) are now married to Crandell and Duran.

Incredibly, given how regressive it was even at the time the film was made, *Operation Petticoat* was made into a TV series in 1977 for ABC television. A slicker and less vulgar version of British TV's equally sexist *On the Buses*, it, like its British cousin, deserved little but an inglorious death and eternal oblivion thereafter, and has on the whole received it.

Two decades later, in a 'post-feminist' culture, the submarine genre began to grapple seriously with the presence of women, real and

Cary Grant and Joan
O'Brien in *Operation
Petticoat*.

fictional. In *Below*, the sudden and involuntary intrusion of one woman on to the troubled USS *Tiger Shark* – Olivia Williams's sole British nurse survivor of an earlier incident – is nearly as disruptive as the vengeful ghost stalking the boat. In an ironic inversion of the hand-held camera rush through the boat pioneered by *Das Boot*, the news of the presence of a woman – a 'skirt' and a 'bleeder'– on board rockets through the submarine and profoundly unsettles the men, overtly connecting her alien perspective/sexual difference with the chthonic chaos of the murdered captain's unquiet spirit.

The explosion of female sexuality into the constricted world of the submarine can have liberating effects. Sophie Walton's series of erotic short stories, *Steampunk Submarine* (2012–15), mixes, in its own words, 'hot women in Victorian underwear and hosiery, a 400 ft submarine, rubber fetish, restraint, breath control and lots of passionate lesbian sex.' Given steampunk's fashion sense, so heavily laced with the tropes of Victorian erotica such as corsets, stockings and lace-up boots (with goggles and holsters thrown in for good measure), it is surprising it took so long to transplant its fetishized sexuality to the submarine.

Walton's stories are pornography, but unlike the male-centric, sexist stereotypes in the works of writers such as Clancy and Robinson, they have strong leading female characters and a lusty honesty. In Clancy and his ilk there is never any real, physical sex of any kind, simply a twee sexism, a passionless dream of 1950s America with twenty-first-century technology for the boys to play with.

Patrick Robinson is much happier to simply objectify women. Throughout ten submarine-themed techno-thrillers written between 1997 and 2008, he confines his female characters to wives or secretaries, with an occasional journalist thrown in briefly. They are invariably physically attractive. Kathy, the secretary of his protagonist Admiral Morgan, is 'spectacularly beautiful', 'the best-looking lady in the White House and possibly the best-looking redhead in Washington'. Despite their age difference, Kathy, who has a tendency to 'sashay' into his office rather than walk, enters into a relationship with the 'still vigorous' 61-year-old Morgan, but will not marry him until he retires. In this she is showing due regard to his awesome responsibilities. 'His other two wives did not, I believe, understand how important he is,' explains Kathy.[6]

Morgan is not the only man to be lucky in his women. 'Boomer' Dunning, the secondary hero of *Kilo Class*, has a wife who has retained her youthful beauty. 'Jo Dunning was a spectacular sight. Her dark red hair, long slim legs, and what Hollywood described as "drop dead looks" somehow betrayed her.' But Jo knows who is even more spectacular, as does Robinson himself:

At 38 years of age she still looked perfect, and she was still dewy-eyed over her husband. She adored even the sight of him in uniform, this handsome, commanding man, about a half inch taller than six feet, blond hair, massive arms and tree-trunk legs. Boomer looked like what he was, an ocean-racing yachtsman when he had the chance, a man who was an America's Cup class sailor, a true son of the sea. His father had been the same, but had left the navy after World War II as a Lieutenant Commander and proceeded to make a great deal of money with a Boston stock broking firm.[7]

Morgan and Dunning are the tip of a deeply self-satisfied male world, one soaked in Republican sexual politics and casual homophobia. Morgan even hates his office phone because it is not bulky and muscular but slim and pastel green, 'a goddamn faggot phone'. Women run the home and worry about their men. Despite repeated assurance of the wives' erotic allure there are no depictions of actual sex between them and their husbands, or sexual encounters of any kind. Sex only exists in reference to producing future or more children, an enjoyable duty for the man, a biological destiny for the woman.

Michael DiMercurio's marital relationships are more complex and fraught, with domestic problems often bedeviling the men at sea and causing them to lose focus. In *Threat Vector* (2000, set in 2018) DiMercurio ventures into territory Clancy and Robinson could barely conceive – a female submarine captain. DiMercurio's acknowledgement of an efficient, capable female submarine officer arose from a change in his views about female submarine crew from long-held opposition to reluctant agreement, after instructing male and female cadets at the U.S. Naval Academy and seeing no disparity between them in talent. He even concludes his assessment of the prospect of introducing women into the USN submarine force, written in 2006, with an emphatic endorsement.

In *Emergency Deep* (2004) he attempted to dramatize the dynamics of having female submarine crew, specifically that of a male captain and a female XO. While the XO, Natalie D'Assault, is characterized as competent and efficient – Captain Dillinger concedes she is a better

xo than he used to be, because she uses psychology and empathy instead
of blunt authority – the relationship between captain and first officer,
both single, is complicated by gender and sexual attraction.

After an embarrassing encounter in the head (toilet and shower)
reserved for captain and xo, the sexual tension between them is only
resolved when the xo makes the first move. In doing so she behaves in
a manner – physical contact at the workplace without prior consent
– that in reverse would constitute sexual harassment by the captain. By
the end captain and xo are engaged to be married, and the intrusion
of a woman, even a professionally competent one, into the male world
of the submarine has been absorbed into more traditional gender roles.
Informing his old friend Pete Vornado of the happy news, the captain
declares, 'You see, this isn't just Lieutenant Commander D'Assault.
You're looking at the future Mrs Burke Dillinger.'[8]

The nods to female submariners in techno-thriller writers like
DiMercurio are positive signs but are undercut by eventual reversion
to accepted gender norms. They do not challenge the genre's basic
instincts. Without exception, heterosexual men remain the default
perspective and the crux of the action. The narratives include no gay
or bisexual men, no lesbians, no feminists and no trans people. While
straight women have belatedly begun to appear, even on board the submarine, they do so in the manner of Rick Campbell's Christine
O'Connor, a no-nonsense national security advisor (a position that
techno-thriller writers seem to think suited to women) who is allowed
to drive substantial portions of the narrative but only in directions laid
down by the genre's militaristic patriotism.

The total exclusion of LGBTQ+ characters from submarine narratives is an accurate mirror of their real-world exclusion from service on
submarines, which has only very recently begun to be addressed and is
still an uncertain process. In 1957 a U.S. Navy board of inquiry conducted a research report, named the Crittenden Report after its author
Captain S. H. Crittenden, into the possible revision of procedures to
manage homosexual personnel in the navy and whether there was a

need to continue the policy of automatic dismissal for gay and bisexual servicemen.

The report concluded that 'the concept that homosexuals necessarily pose a security risk is unsupported by adequate factual data.' Despite these findings, the report recommended no changes to the Navy's dismissal policies, not for reasons related to the efficiency of the service but in order to mirror anti-gay prejudice within American society: 'The service should not move ahead of civilian society nor attempt to set substantially different standards in attitude or action with respect to homosexual offenders.'[9]

President Clinton's problematic 'Don't Ask, Don't Tell' policy in regards to lesbians, gays and bisexuals in the military was applied from 1993 to 2011, causing as many difficulties as it avoided. In December 2010, after being passed by the House and Senate, President Obama signed the Don't Ask, Don't Tell Repeal Act 2010 into law. Under its provisions any restrictions on service in the U.S. military applying to gays, lesbians and bisexuals ended as of 20 September 2011.

The issue had more resonance within the submarine service, given its nature and working environment, than in the other branches of the military. In no other part of the military are groups of (ostensibly) straight men confined together in such close and intimate proximity. Inevitably they form a social group. One of the highlights of a mission of an American SSBN is 'Halfway Night', a raucous party held at the halfway point of the voyage, where the usual formalities between officers and ratings are allowed to lapse for the occasion.

No one would suggest this becomes a sexual bacchanal but the connotations of the event – a close group of young men in uniform partying together in an industrial confined space – cannot be entirely absent from the minds of those participating, especially as the close confines of submarine life mean that sexual release, that is, masturbation, is rarely private. One of the codes of submarine service is that if the closed curtain of a seaman's bunk is 'rocking', the occupant should not be disturbed.

Bunks in a u.s. Navy submarine.

Interviewed in 2016, an experienced ship's diver and fire control technician who served on American SSNs from 2000 to 2010 recalls one occasion when sexual release was virtually a communal event:

> I was one of the divers on the boats so I had to secure every-thing topside before we submerged. I'm always the last guy to go down. We had literally just gotten underway. As soon as you get underway everyone turns off the lights and people try to start getting some sleep. I went down into the crew's berthing, and it's basically just a really narrow hallway with rack after rack after rack, and I flipped on the lights and every single curtain was rocking, and I just screamed 'Oh my god, you guys couldn't wait an hour?' and all of a sudden it just kinda stopped.[10]

On the surface (both literally and metaphorically) submariners are keen to deny prejudice against LGBTQ+ people. The personal memoirs of submariners, found in book or blog or interview, insist that the main obstacles to the free expression of gay sexuality within a submarine is space and privacy rather than the innate prejudice of their colleagues. Reflecting on the homophobic joke told by the other services of the submarine force – '160 men go down, 80 couples come up', or as the force itself has it, 'It's not gay if you're underway' – a USN submarine officer wrote:

> Whatever, man. We had some gay guys onboard *and nobody cared*. We cared more that they did their jobs. What they did in their personal life is no one's business. I never heard about any guys getting it on underway. And remember about the lack of personal space. Two people sneaking off to fuck are going to get caught. There's no place to hide.[11]

Were it not the case that homosexuality simply has no space or opportunity to overtly express itself on board a submarine, it is unlikely that attitudes among male submariners who overwhelmingly identify as heterosexual would be quite as relaxed as this idealistic account implies. The 2015 case of an openly gay submariner on the SSN USS *Florida* who was subject to relentless 'hazing' (derogatory jokes, being referred to as 'Brokeback', crude cartoons left on his locker) that led eventually to the dismissal of the chief of the boat for failing to intervene or inform the captain, suggests so.[12] These attitudes feed into submarine fiction. The problematic nature of masculinity itself is seldom (actually never) addressed within the genre, much less the unquestioned primacy of heterosexuality.

Yet these rules are not laws of physics. There is no inherent reason why the genre's narrative conventions should bar a suitably dramatized story of same-sex attraction, something the long history of gay relationships in the military – from Alexander and Hephaestion to George Melly's Rabelaisian memoir of 'rum, bum and concertina' in the British Navy of the 1940s – would support. These relationships vary in their frequency, meaning and intensity, from casual seamen's encounters to the regular visits made by Lord Mountbatten and other British naval officers to the Red House, an exclusive gay brothel in Rabat, Malta, during the 1950s.[13] Such scenarios could, if suitably and sensitively dramatized, form the basis of powerful narratives about the suppression of homoerotic desire within a culture of very traditional masculinity.

It was only in 2021, with BBC's *Vigil*, that the gender and sexual conventions of the genre were challenged. The emotional core of *Vigil's* narrative is the romantic relationship between police detective Amy Silva (Suranne Jones), sent to investigate a murder on board a Vanguard-class submarine, and her younger partner Kirsten Longacre (Rose Leslie), conducting the investigation on land. Not only is the relationship sensitively and realistically handled (Amy, who self-identified as straight and has a daughter from a prior heterosexual relationship, is confused and unsettled by her attraction to Kirsten) but it is central to the plot as messages sent between them draw on their intimacy for code words they do not want others to understand. Placing a same-sex relationship at the centre of a prime-time submarine-themed political thriller was an audacious move that brilliantly subverted the genre's historic sexual politics.

The submarine genre, like all art and fiction, moves with the times and with shifts in social attitudes. Where it leads and occasionally forms those attitudes, it is in accounts of scientific and technological exploration rather than in those of personal and sexual relations. In some ways the older classics of the genre, being less concerned with making a political statement, were more liberal than its modern variant, even though the nature of their narratives often meant there were few female characters and no LGBTQ+ ones.

For all that, the 'social realist' submarine authors of the post-war world, such as Reeman and Fullerton, made some attempt to flesh out the domestic and emotional lives of their protagonists by adding significant scenes on shore or in flashbacks. Fullerton even devoted an entire novel, *A Wren Called Smith* (1957), to a female protagonist, albeit one whose unwitting sexual attraction caused havoc in the emotional lives of male submarine officers and captured POWs. In the 1990s he branched out entirely with his 'Rosie Ewing' series, the adventures of a female SOE agent in Nazi-occupied France.

Some of this work, novels and stories outside the cold fetishistic tracklines of the modern American techno-thriller, showed men who were not always predictably masculine and women who had other qualities than the physical. In contrast to the casual sexism of Clancy, Robinson and their ilk, Commander Beach, the author of *Run Silent, Run Deep*, when discussing the writing process, including the depiction of female characters, had the self-knowledge to frankly admit,

> Things have to happen, one thing happens after another. All of a sudden you come to an impasse, and you throw it away and start over again. The subs I did okay, but writing about women – I never had so much trouble in my life as with that one.[14]

CONCLUSION:
THE END OF THE SUBMARINE?

In 2018 the submarine genre received an unexpected accolade that demonstrated, if nothing else, its continuing power over the popular mind. In that year the American Public Broadcasting Service (PBS), after extensive public consultation as part of its *The Great American Read* project, announced 'the 100 most-loved books in the U.S.'. Number one was Harper Lee's *To Kill a Mockingbird*, with other predictable classics such as *Pride and Prejudice, Little Women, The Great Gatsby* and *The Grapes of Wrath* high on the list. At number 59 was Tom Clancy's *The Hunt for Red October*.

This is dismaying, and not only because *Red October*, like all of Clancy's work, has almost no literary merit. If the right-wing techno-porn served up by Clancy and his heirs is the future of the fictional submarine genre, it scarcely deserves to have one. It would be regrettable, though, if this were to be the genre's enduring legacy when it contains a finer tradition epitomized by writers like Verne, Fullerton, Reeman and Bucheim, and by films such as *Men Without Women, Morning Departure, Das Boot, Crimson Tide* and *Black Sea*.

Despite this record the submarine genre has produced no literary classics, only a handful of essential films, and just one supreme work of art – *Das Boot*, both Buchheim's novel and Petersen's film. It is the product *par excellence* of popular culture, expressed either as historical fiction, political thriller or pulp SF, all genres marginalized by the professional guardians of high culture. From *Nautilus* to *Kursk*, the genre

Model of Naval Group's concept SMX-31 submarine, displayed at Euronaval 2018 in Le Bourget, near Paris.

has moved in lockstep with the global military-industrial complex. The next iteration of submarines will lay new tracks for it to follow.

A possible future for the real-world submarine was unveiled at the 2018 Paris Euronaval Exhibition in the revolutionary design schematics for the prototype SMX-31. If built, the SMX submarine would have no conning tower, retractable hydro-planes that fold into the hull, a hexagonal patterned skin with built-in sensors and propulsor pump jets in its stern. Its rotating photonic masts will send visual images to large-screen displays in the ship's control room via fibre optics (the U.S. Navy's Virginia-class submarines, the French Navy's Suffren-class submarines and some of Russia's Borei-class submarines already possess photonic masts). Powered by lithium-ion batteries, and with a maximum crew of fifteen, the SMX would be to the standard diesel-electric and SSN submarine what the stealth bomber is to the Lancaster.[1]

Running parallel to these new designs are equally innovative anti-submarine warfare technologies. Foremost among these are the U.S. Navy's SQQ-89 Combat System, which utilizes Synthetic Aperture Sonar more sensitive to acoustic pings than standard sonar, and the P-8A Poseidon sub-hunting airplane, armed with gyro-stabilized image intensifiers and infrared sensors that are able to detect a submarine from high altitude.

China's ASW is even more ambitious. The Chinese Navy's Project Guanlan is on the point of advancing Light Detection and Ranging (Lidar) technology to such an extent that an orbiting satellite, firing high-powered laser pulses in different colours and frequencies over a specific area of ocean, could detect a submarine even at a depth of 500 metres (1,640 ft).[2] In addition to a range of new 'quieting technologies' to help its submarines avoid detection, the People's Liberation Army Navy (PLAN) is currently developing 'large, smart, and relatively low-cost unmanned submarines that can roam the world's oceans to perform a wide range of missions'. In 2018 the *South China Morning Post* revealed that the PLAN's high-priority, hitherto secret Project 912 aimed to develop a new generation of submarines run purely by AI.[3]

Considering these and similar technological developments, a 2015 report by the Washington-based Center for Strategic and Budgetary Assessments (CSBA) concluded that the submarine of the twenty-first century will 'shift from being front-line tactical platforms like aircraft to being host and co-ordination platforms like aircraft carriers.'[4] In other words, future submarines may not actually engage in combat or even enter combat zones, but merely deliver advanced weapons packages that do. Even the narco-submarines used by Colombian drug traffickers in the 'Transit Zone' – an expanse of ocean that includes the Caribbean Sea, the Gulf of Mexico and the eastern Pacific – will shortly become remote-controlled, removing the need to surface for air and so making interdiction by law enforcement agencies more difficult.[5]

The metamorphosis of the world's submarine force is not confined to the military. Civilian-controlled nuclear submarines, which have the latitude to replace torpedo tubes and missile launch systems with robotic exploration hardware and autonomous sub-sea vehicles, are being developed by both America and Russia. These submarines have great potential use in monitoring ice cores, ocean temperatures and water salinity and in helping research and develop alternative, sustainable energy sources to replace fossil fuels.

It would take only a modicum of imagination and dramatic licence to incorporate these vessels and their scientific research missions into the fictional submarine genre, adding fresh narrative juice, gender diversity and ecological politics to the standard tropes of the submarine adventure, shaking matters up considerably. Alas, with the sole exception of TV's *Vigil* the genre continues to rely on formulaic military thrillers like *Hunter Killer*. Better films such as *Kursk* explore the lethal hazards of submarine service, although are hardly the first to do so. But the first great popular film centred on climate change, in which a submarine and its research work could play a pivotal role, has yet to appear.

Whether research performed by submarines proves beneficial or not will depend on the extent to which political and democratic pressure can force governments to adopt long-term, ecologically sustainable energy policies that move away from reliance on fossil fuels. This will be difficult to achieve. Russia, for example, is ramping up economic development of its Arctic territories, including new oil and natural gas fields on the Yamal Peninsula. It is now predicted that by the mid-2030s global warming will make the Arctic Ocean completely ice-free in summer. By 2050 it may be ice free all year round. The use of a new generation of research submarines to explore an ice-free Arctic and assist in sub-sea extraction of oil and gas will very likely contribute to escalating climate change and have disastrous long-term consequences.

Regardless of the use to which they are put, positive or negative, the development of fully automated submarines will spell the end of the Earth-bound fictional submarine genre. There are no SF novels about unmanned missions to Mars. Even *Accelerando* (2005), Charles Stross's radically unsettling novel of the Singularity – the point beyond which ICT and AI produce a world that biological humanity can no longer control or comprehend – grounded his tale in the personality patterns of actual people, transplanted to chips in a matchbox-sized exploratory vessel in deep space.

Submarines themselves are less transferable. While the obvious first bases for human colonies – the Moon and Mars – have no oceans, and other planets are simply too inhospitable, Jupiter's moon Europa is an intriguing option. It has a water-ice crust and a thin oxygen atmosphere, and the heat from Jupiter keeps Europa's oceans from freezing. Many scientists consider it may contain extra-terrestrial life, which might be discovered by a suitably equipped submersible or submarine discovery mission. NASA's Europa Lander, due to launch in 2024 to arrive at Europa in 2030, where it will search for bio-signatures, could initiate such a programme.

Saturn's moon Titan may be even more receptive to submarine exploration. Titan is the only world in our solar system, beyond Earth, known to host stable bodies of liquid on its surface: great hydrocarbon lakes of liquid methane and ethane that are larger than North America's

Great Lakes. In 2016 NASA's Innovative Advanced Concepts (NIAC) programme, which seeks to jump-start potentially game-changing exploration ideas and technologies, provided grants to draw up an engineering blueprint for a submarine to be used on Titan.

The Europa and Titan projects suggest an exciting new direction not only for submarine exploration but for the submarine genre itself. Even if the next iteration of Earth's submarine technology is the unmanned and robotic vessel, inherently difficult to dramatize, the underlying themes and tropes of the genre will endure as these blueprints and prototypes advance. Although historical re-enactment dramas such as *The Hunley* and *U-571* will continue to be made, and may yet offer something new within their set paradigms, the main genre will in all probability slowly morph into a sub-set of SF.

It is a process that has been underway for some time. *Alien* (dir. Ridley Scott, 1979) is essentially a submarine film set in deep space, drenched in the genre's industrial aesthetic and visceral claustrophobia. *Apollo 13* (dir. Ron Howard, 1995) ticks every box of the submarine-in-peril story – a small vessel far from base, desperate efforts to stay alive inside a sophisticated tin can, and an environment utterly lethal to human life just outside the hull. *Life* (dir. Daniel Espinosa, 2017) does much the same, although its immediate threat is a parasitic Martian lifeform rather than mechanical malfunction.

This mashed-up genre is adaptable, as the steely, cerebral TV reboot of *Battlestar Galactica* (2003–8) demonstrated. When the artificial Cylons annihilate humanity's 'Thirteen Colonies', the *Galactica* is the only survivor of its large space fleet. A functional weapon of interstellar war, built for survival rather than comfort, the *Galactica* must provide protection to a rag-tag collection of private and commercial starships while leading a desperate search for 'Earth', the Colonies' legendary home planet. Where the *Enterprise* of *Star Trek: The Next Generation* is an elegant flagship engaged primarily in scientific and diplomatic missions, comfortably part of a wider society and only periodically in real danger, the *Galactica* is a hunted submarine.

That the submarine genre can easily transfer from its birthing pool, that is, Earth's oceans, to the larger ocean of space underlines its continuing attraction and relevance. The archetypal potency and sexual symbolism of the submarine is obvious. It is a death-dealing Jungian nightmare, a dark-grey phallic symbol that only women or hippies would paint pink or yellow. It cleaves the depths of Mother Earth, manned by hard-boiled men fully primed to shoot their load in apocalyptic climax.

The professionalism and courage of those who serve inside submarines is not in question. But courage is amoral. The men on the *Hunley* died for slavery, those in the U-boats for fascism. If ordered to, the crews of the SSBNs fetishized by Clancy, Robinson and Campbell would unleash Armageddon without a qualm (the refusal of *Crimson Tide*'s XO to endorse an order to fire nuclear missiles is because he believes a countermanding order has been relayed but not received, not because he would not fire them if properly ordered to).

Discourse, factual and fictional, is crucial to the future of the submarine. Although major strategic decisions invariably follow state priorities, those priorities can be influenced and redirected. In societies whose ruling elites must attend to the *vox populi*, if only to retain their power and privilege, the quality, scope and honesty of discourse can be important.

If that discourse is a parade of militaristic techno-thrillers about the adrenalin-pumping, life-saving properties of the latest high-tech hunter killer attack submarine – as in Rick Campbell's *Deep Strike* (2021), in which a rogue Russian SSBN controlled by ISIS threatens to annihilate America's East Coast unless prevented by a swift SSN counter-attack – it will leave its audience as eager to comply with the next war fever as were the masses of Europe in August 1914. If, however, it has greater variety, integrity, imagination and scepticism, if it suggests that the mighty 'boomer' of submarine legend is a politically and morally bankrupt machine, that a submarine's better use would be in exploring human and marine science, then strategy and budgetary plans could shift.

For example, if the UK's Trident nuclear deterrent programme was to be scrapped and the submarines that carry it decommissioned, the £205 billion saved over thirty years could in theory be redirected to eliminate child poverty in the UK, build over one hundred new hospitals, employ 150,000 additional nurses, build 3 million affordable homes, install solar panels in every home in the UK and be used to counter genuine threats to national security and well-being such as climate change and cyber-terrorism.[6]

The funds released would be large enough to regenerate entire regions such as Barrow-in-Furness, Cumbria, the centre of submarine production in the UK and now entirely dependent on one industry and one huge defence contractor. The Dreadnought-class submarines that will carry the next generation of ICBMs – commonly referred to as the 'Successor' programme – are being constructed at the Barrow shipyard by BAE Systems, the UK economy's single largest manufacturer.

The designs for the Dreadnought-class submarines emerged from BAE's cavernous 'Blue Lagoon' facility, where for the first time the engineering schematics for the SSBNs were not drawn up on paper by hundreds of skilled draughtsman but by 3D Computer-Aided Design (CAD) software. Echoing the 'partnership' between the UK and the USA laid down by Admiral Rickover in 1958, which guarantees a hefty slice of the action to American business, the design process is abetted through a permanent secure link between Barrow and the General Dynamics facility at Groton, Connecticut. The technological and design skills involved are impressive, but aside from providing high-quality employment for 3,000 workers in Barrow, to what end?

In order to provide more options for the region's workers and to move British industry away from an unhealthy over-reliance on arms manufacturing, Unite, the trade union that represents the bulk of the Barrow workforce, has been attempting to promote debate about a realistic programme of defence diversification. The Labour Party has adopted some of these ideas as part of a 'Green New Deal' for British industry, pledging that jobs lost through the cancellation of

Dreadnought or non-renewal of Trident would be replaced with high-skilled employment in renewable energy such as solar, wind and wave power. This message needs to cut through to the public, most especially to the workforce affected.

The sanitization, even domestication, of the nuclear submarine reached surreal levels with the Royal Navy's efforts to add colourful interior decor to its fleet. From the 1960s to the 1990s the MOD commissioned the Sanderson company, owner of the Morris & Co. brand, to supply William Morris's *Rose* fabric design for some of the interiors (such as bunk curtains, pillows and seat covers) of its nuclear submarines, including SSBNs carrying Trident missiles. The *Rose* fabric was 'the only point where nature, however stylised, is represented on any significant scale and the only point where fabric is used to soften the experience of living inside the machine'.[7]

The fabric was used only in the officers' and senior ratings' mess and sleeping areas, not those of the rest of the crew. Yet the essence of Morris's artistic philosophy, expounded in essays such as 'How We Live and How We Might Live' (1884) and 'Useful Work versus Useless Toil' (1885), was that art should be an organic part of everyday life, that it should emerge from and complement the life of artisans and workers. He was a passionate anti-war campaigner and critic of British imperialism, a civilian Captain Nemo wielding a radical pen and voice instead of a submarine. It is impossible to imagine a greater perversion of his values than the use of his work to adorn select quarters aboard a state-sponsored weapon of mass destruction.

The Morris fabric's placement on board the UK's SSBNs featured prominently in the 'Material Nuclear Culture' exhibition at the Karst Gallery, Plymouth, in 2016, which aimed to explore the 'material traces and cultural legacy' of nuclear-powered submarines in the UK. The publicity for the exhibition, which included a round-table discussion among artists, submariners and members of the MOD's Submarine Dismantling Project Advisory Group, explained:

This year will mark the end of the Royal Navy fifteen-year public consultation on how to dismantle British nuclear submarines, and where to store the reactor vessels. The Submarine Dismantling Project Advisory Group is the first MOD public consultation with expert advisors, NGOs and statutory agencies that represent a range of experience and political concerns. The exhibition takes place in the spirit of the advisory group and their commitment to an open and frank discussion about the issues of nuclear dismantling and radioactive waste management.[8]

As part of the Material Nuclear Culture project the artist David Mabb visited HMS *Courageous*, which saw action in the Falklands War and, following its decommission in 1992, is now open to the public in Plymouth. Following the visit Mabb created the art installation 'A Provisional Memorial to Nuclear Disarmament', used in the exhibition and later on display at Kelmscott House. Mabb's work interfused the *Rose* pattern with anti-nuclear iconography, protest banners and quotations from E. P. Thompson's *William Morris: Romantic to Revolutionary* to provoke questions about the use of art in the nuclear age, and to reclaim the original intent of Morris's work.

It is unlikely the MOD either knew or cared that Thompson, Morris's greatest biographer, was the founder of European Nuclear Disarmament (END) and one of the most active opponents of Polaris and Trident. Writing of the nuclear escalation of the early 1980s between the USA and the USSR, Thompson's analysis is still relevant today, particularly his rallying cry to all those who wish to actively campaign against the weapons of nuclear holocaust:

Finally, it should go without saying that exterminism can only be confronted by the broadest possible popular alliance: that is, by every affirmative resource in our culture. Secondary differences must be subordinated to the human ecological imperative

... Those voices which pipe, in shrill tones of militancy, that 'the Bomb' is 'a class question'; that we must get back to the dramas of confrontation and spurn the contamination of Christians, neutralists, pacifists and other class enemies – these voices are only a falsetto descant in the choir of exterminism. Only an alliance which takes in churches, Euro-Communists, Labourists,

Drone delivering payload to the ballistic missile submarine USS *Henry M. Jackson* around the Hawaiian Islands, October 2020.

East European dissidents, Soviet citizens unmediated by Party structures, trade unionists, ecologists –only this can possibly muster the force and the internationalist elan to throw the cruise missiles and the ss-20s back.[9]

Little has changed since the Second Cold War. The kind of broad-based, nonsectarian alliance that Thompson called for is even more necessary now. Its moral basis is unanswerable and has been restated by those official representatives of Christianity who believe in translating their faith into reality. In May 2019, when a National Service of Thanksgiving to mark fifty years of British nuclear weapons being on constant patrol at sea was held in Westminster Abbey, the Bishop of Colchester declined to attend, writing in the *New Statesman*: 'The Church of England has a duty to stand up as a force for peace in our communities and for the flourishing of all humanity. It cannot do so if it celebrates, even tacitly, nuclear weapons.'

Over two hundred Anglican clerics signed a Christian CND statement opposing the thanksgiving service on the grounds that the Church of England Synod has called on Christians to 'work tirelessly' to eliminate nuclear weapons, not to host a service praising their deployment, and that the UK government was obliged under the Nuclear Non-Proliferation Treaty to enter into negotiations to curtail them.[10] It follows that if the UK's nuclear missiles are to be eliminated, then the only remaining vehicles for their delivery, nuclear-powered submarines, will have to be either decommissioned or converted to civilian use.

Given current political trends it is probable that the nuclear submarine, rather than becoming a benign undersea version of the electric car, will continue to threaten the biosphere and all life upon it. Unlike the socially progressive use of technology postulated in utopias such as that of Aaron Bastani's *Fully Automated Luxury Communism* (2019), automated AI submarines will be even more capable than the older generation of submarines of unleashing a nuclear holocaust. Their programmes will contain not the slightest hesitation or doubt about an order to fire.

Yet the threat posed by the nuclear arms race, at its most intense in the continued development of SSBNs and their payloads, is increasingly perceived as somehow a 'second order' problem, as if it is simply too vast and awful to contemplate. While campaigning bodies like CND and Code Pink continue to valiantly oppose nuclear escalation and highlight to what better use the astronomical sums involved could be put, the fervour and fear surrounding the issue does not appear to match that of the 1980s.

Faced with so many existential horrors, the majority of political activists prefer to put their energies into fighting the terminal cancer of climate change or the social poison of massive wealth inequality rather than the ticking time bomb of nuclear war. Meanwhile the SSNs and SSBNs continue to roll out of China's Huludao submarine factory, Trident is now to be renewed, India and Russia are expanding their nuclear submarine fleets, and covert submersibles such as the Status-6 inch closer to enemy shores.

These are powerful scenarios but they do not make for enduring art. Nor do they provide much space for careful and sensitive delineation of character. The submarine genre, for all its potency and relevance to an increasingly dangerous twenty-first-century world, continues to lack a Patrick O'Brian. Kipling's efforts aside, it missed immortalization by the great war poets. It has yet to produce a *Sword of Honour* trilogy or a *Catch-22*, although Buchheim's *Das Boot* deserves inclusion in the literary canon.

And yet, with all these limitations, the submarine has carved a distinctive mark on our culture and our psyche. Like its subject, it is one that is rarely seen whole and is often disregarded. Where the tank and the fighter jet arrogantly strut their stuff, crushing opposition and demanding attention, the submarine is mostly seen at rest in dock or moving through a placid sea. Occasionally it surfaces through an ice pack, sitting incongruously at the planet's poles. Its active self is a hidden thing, moving through the deep and waiting for its moment, tended by devoted crews operating to esoteric codes and secret arcana.

From the *Hunley* to the SMX, the submarine has come a long way and its mission is not yet complete. At some point it may have its Battle of Kursk. But even that may not be the end. SF is replete with scenarios where the ultimate in iconic military kit is found lying naked in the desert or roving around a dying world. One thing is certain, in life and in art: whatever finally destroys humanity – a pandemic, a comet strike, a rogue AI, uncontrollable climate change or nuclear war – when all is lost and urban civilization lies in ruins, what will remain of us, for a brief time at least, will be the submarine.

REFERENCES

INTRODUCTION: THE IMAGE OF A SUBMARINE

1 Philip Zeigler, *Mountbatten: The Official Biography* (New York, 1985), p. 557.
2 Margaret Drabble, 'Submarine Dreams: Jules Verne's Twenty Thousand Leagues Under the Seas', *New Statesman*, www.newstatesman.com, 8 May 2014.
3 'Submarine Memes for the New Millennium', https://theleansubmariner.com, accessed 1 November 2018.
4 Iain Sinclair, *London Overground: A Day's Walk Around the Ginger Line* (London, 2015), p. 235.

1 THE SUBMARINE IN WAR

1 There is dispute about exactly who discovered the wreck of the *Hunley*. The underwater archaeologist E. Lee Spence claims to have discovered the wreck in 1970, and even had its location included on the U.S. National Register of Historic Places in 1978. Mutual lawsuits by Spence and Cussler against each other were dropped, and so there was no final, definitive legal ruling on their respective claims. The most reasonable conclusion is that Spence made an extremely good approximation of where the *Hunley* might be and even published a book in January 1995 with a helpful map to its location, without which Cussler's team could not have found it in April 1995. Cussler should not have claimed that the find was entirely new when his NUMA team had basically verified Spence's discovery. However, that discovery was speculative, and it is unlikely that the *Hunley* would have been raised and restored without the publicity attracted by the NUMA operation.
2 Iain Ballantyne, *The Deadly Trade: The Complete History of Submarine Warfare from Archimedes to the Present* (London, 2018), p. 73.
3 HMS *Holland 1* is now on display at the Royal Navy Submarine Museum, Gosport, across the Solent from Portsmouth Historic Dockyard.
4 Brayton Harris and Walter J. Boyne, ed., *The Navy Times Book of Submarines: A Political, Social, and Military History* (New York, 1997), p. 176.

5 Howard Zinn, *A People's History of the United States* (New York, 2003), pp. 362–3.
6 Len Deighton, *Blood, Tears and Folly: An Objective Look at World War II* (London, 1993), p. 15.
7 Siegfried Sassoon, 'Base Details', in *The Penguin Book of First World War Poetry*, ed. Jon Silkin (London, 1979), p. 131.
8 Andrew Roberts, *The Storm of War: A New History of the Second World War* (London, 2010), pp. 351–74.
9 Deighton, *Blood, Tears and Folly*, p. 27.
10 Ibid., p. 31.
11 The 'Citadel' is still there, an ugly and enigmatic block of concrete covered in Virginia creeper that overlooks Horse Guards Parade. It is unclear exactly what its current function is but it would be surprising if it did not provide access to a nuclear bunker for the staff of the Cabinet Office, to which it is attached.
12 Roberts, *The Storm of War*, p. 368.
13 Edward S. Miller, *War Plan Orange: The U.S. Strategy to Defeat Japan, 1897–1945* (Annapolis, MD, 1991), p. 320.
14 Matthew Robert McGrew, 'Beneath the Surface: American Culture and Submarine Warfare in the Twentieth Century', Master's Thesis, University of Southern Mississippi (2011), available in *Master's Theses*, 209, https://aquila.usm.edu, p. 71.
15 J. T. McDaniel, 'Run Silent, Run Deep', www.jtmcdaniel.com, accessed 28 May 2021.
16 Lothar-Günther Buchheim and J. Maxwell Brownjohn, trans., *U-Boat* (London, 1976), p. 118.
17 Ibid., p. 134.
18 Joe Kennedy, *Authentocrats: Culture, Politics and the New Seriousness* (London, 2018), pp. 117–18.
19 Tyler Rogoway, 'Confessions of a U.S. Navy Submarine Officer', *Jalopnik*, https://jalopnik.com, 2 July 2015.

2 THE SUBMARINE IN POLITICS

1 Peter Hennessy and James Jinks, *The Silent Deep: The Royal Navy Submarine Service since 1945* (London, 2015), p. 45.
2 Mark Kennard and Mark Curtis, 'Britain's Warfare State', www.opendemocracy.net, 24 September 2018.
3 Sir Arthur Conan Doyle, 'The Adventure of the Bruce-Partington Plans', in *Sherlock Holmes: The Complete Novels and Stories*, vol. II, ed. Loren D. Estleman (New York, 1986), pp. 398–427.
4 Fullerton obtained design details of the fictional *E-57* (Britain only built 56 E-class submarines) and its operating procedures from builders' plans

in the National Maritime Museum, Greenwich; from *General Orders for Submarines 1913, Notes for Officers under Instruction November 1918*; and from an old E-class crewlist and watchbill, all of which are available at the Submarine Museum, Gosport.

5 Alexander Fullerton, *Patrol to the Golden Horn* (New York, 2001), p. 68.

6 Ibid., p. 29.

7 See Iain Ballantyne, *The Deadly Trade: The Complete History of Submarine Warfare from Archimedes to the Present* (London, 2018), pp. 232–6 for details of this covert operation.

8 The United States's policy towards the Soviet Union and its overall Cold War strategy of massively increased defence spending allied to political and economic subversion of progressive nationalist regimes that might be sympathetic to the Soviet Union is contained in the National Security Council (NSC) memorandum 68, dated 14 April 1950, in *Naval War College Review*, XXVII/6 (1975), pp. 51–108.

9 Hennessy and Jinks, *The Silent Deep*, p. 325.

10 *Take 'Er Down* (dir. U.S. Navy, 1954)

11 Hennessy and Jinks, *The Silent Deep*, p. 150.

12 For details of these two incidents/missions, see Hennessy and Jinks, *The Silent Deep*, pp. 342–3, and Tom Clancy, *Submarine: A Guided Tour Inside a Nuclear Warship* (New York, 1988), pp. 215–16.

13 Stuart Prebble, *Secrets of the Conqueror: The Untold Story of Britain's Most Famous Submarine* (London, 2012), p. 87.

14 It is popular mythology that *The Sun*'s notorious headline had an exclamation mark for emphasis – GOTCHA! – but the paper's front page on 30 May 1982 shows this was not the case. This does not make it any less of a bloodthirsty display by armchair warriors.

15 Thatcher was lucky in the timing and outcome of the Falklands War, and certainly exploited it shamelessly, but the theory that she deliberately torpedoed not only the *Belgrano* but an imminent peace settlement is not as solid as the Left assumes. By 2 May the Peruvian ceasefire proposal had not been conveyed to London. The sinking of the *Belgrano* was not in defiance of the strict terms of the TEZ or Article 51 of the UN Charter. Even after the sinking and the Argentine retaliatory attack on the British destroyer HMS *Sheffield*, sunk with many casualties, the UK government indicated it would sign the ceasefire agreement. The Argentine junta rejected the proposal.

16 Steven Berkoff, *Sink the Belgrano!* (London, 1987), p. 1.

17 Clancy, *Submarine*, p. 147.

18 Yingjie Gu and Matt Sussis, 'Beneath the Surface, a Quiet Superpower Race for Nuclear Supremacy', *USA Today*, 30 June 2018.

19 Robert Hutchinson, *Jane's Submarines: War Beneath the Waves from 1776 to the Present Day* (New York, 2001), p. 132.

20 Patrick Robinson, *Kilo Class* (New York, 1998), pp. 56–7.

21 Christy Tillery French, 'Interview with Michael DiMercurio',
    www.terminalrun.com, accessed 28 May 2021.

22 Michael DiMercurio, *Phoenix Sub Zero* (New York, 1995), p. 18.

23 Tom Clancy, *The Hunt for Red October* (New York, 1985), p. 441.

24 Kyle Mizokami, 'China Is Building the World's Largest Submarine Factory',
    Popular Mechanics, www.popularmechanics.com, 24 April 2017.

25 'India Kickstarts Process to Build 6 Nuclear-Powered Attack Submarines',
    Economic Times, 1 December 2017.

26 Campaign for Nuclear Disarmament, 'MOD Can't Pay £205 Billion
    for Trident? Expect Further Cuts to Schools and Hospitals',
    https://cnduk.org, 19 December 2017.

27 James Goldrick, 'Why Does Australia Need Submarines At All?',
    The Conversation, https://theconversation.com, 28 April 2016.

28 Ballantyne, *The Deadly Trade*, p. 602.

3 THE SUBMARINE AND CATASTROPHE

1   The 'Alpha and Omega' cobalt bomb in *Beneath the Planet of the Apes*
    (1970, dir. Ted Post) is a doomsday device designed to destroy Earth in one
    explosion, worshipped in ignorance by the mutated remains of mankind
    in the ruins of New York, and triggered at the climax of the film by the
    astronaut Taylor in sheer disgust at what has become of his home planet.

2   For the Doomsday Clock see 'Welcome to "The New Abnormal"', *Bulletin
    of the Atomic Scientists*, https://thebulletin.org, 24 January 2019.

3   The Soviet Union's rejoinder to the USA demands that it withdraw its
    missiles from Cuba was that the United States had stationed its own nuclear
    missiles on the Soviet border, specifically in Turkey. It demanded these be
    withdrawn at the same time, something Kennedy never publicly agreed to
    but was willing to concede in back-channel negotiations.

4   Fidel Castro later confirmed that Cuban forces had tactical nuclear warheads
    attached to their artillery rockets and 11-28 bombers and would have fired
    them had Cuba been attacked.

5   Iain Ballantyne, *The Deadly Trade: The Complete History of Submarine
    Warfare from Archimedes to the Present* (London, 2018), p. 531.

6   The November class was not badly built, but it suffered from poor
    maintenance and inadequate refitting. The Soviet Navy's Northern Fleet,
    in particular, had a poor accident record.

7   Benjamin B. Weybrew, *Report Number 917: History of Military Psychology
    at the U.S. Naval Submarine Medical Research Laboratory* (Groton, CT, 1979),
    p. iii.

8   Ibid., p. 11.

9   Edmund N. Epstein, 'Effects of the Cuban Crisis Upon Attitudes Related
    to War and Peace', *Psychological Reports*, XVII/2 (1965) pp. 424–6.

10 For an account of how Able Archer 83 almost led to nuclear war, see Tom Nichols, 'Five Ways Nuclear Armageddon Was Almost Unleashed', *National Interest*, https://nationalinterest.org, 9 August 2014.

11 Anna Russell, 'What Submarine Crews and Astronauts Can Teach Us About Isolation', *New Yorker*, 9 April 2020.

12 Edward Thompson, 'Notes on Exterminism, the Last Stage of Civilization', *New Left Review*, I/121 (1980).

13 Peter Hennessy and James Jinks, *The Silent Deep: The Royal Navy Submarine Service since 1945* (London, 2015), p. 395.

14 Ibid., p. 67.

15 For the Nuclear Control Orders of the U.S. Joint Chiefs of Staff, see 'Emergency Action Procedures of the Joint Chiefs of Staff: Nuclear Control Orders (U)', EAP-JCS, vol. V, 20 March 1985, archived from the original at https://web.archive.org.

16 Ibid.

17 Saman Javed, 'Trump's Withdrawal from Missile Treaty could Escalate U.S. Tensions with China, Experts Warn', *The Independent*, www.independent.co.uk, 23 October 2018.

18 Kyle Mizokami, 'How Russia's New Doomsday Torpedo Works', *Popular Mechanics*, www.popularmechanics.com, 7 March 2018.

19 Spencer Ackerman, 'Exclusive Pictures: Inside the Navy's Newest Spy Sub', *Wired*, www.wired.com, 30 May 2012.

4 THE SUBMARINE AS EXPLORER

1 Quoted in Jeff VanderMeer, *The Steampunk Bible* (New York, 2011), p. 30.

2 Jules Verne, *Twenty Thousand Leagues Under the Sea* [1870] (London, 2014), pp. 64, 66, 118.

3 Edgar Rice Burroughs, *The Land That Time Forgot* [1918] (New York, 1975), p. 10.

4 Jennifer Frazer, 'Inside the U.S.'s Only Ocean Exploration Ship', *Artful Amoeba (Scientific American)*, https://blogs.scientificamerican.com, 13 February 2017.

5 See 'Ultra-Deep Submersibles', https://tritonsubs.com, accessed 28 May 2021.

6 Andrew Tarantola, 'The Super-Secret "Research" Sub That Helped Win the Cold War', *Gizmodo*, https://gizmodo.com, 15 November 2013.

7 Arthur C. Clarke, *The Ghost from the Grand Banks* (London, 1990).

8 Arthur C. Clarke, *The Deep Range* [1957] (London, 1968).

9 James Herbert, *The Dragon in the Sea* (London, 1954), p. 165.

10 Ensign Vigneshwar Manickam, 'Submarines in Space', in *Proceedings of the USNI*, vol. CXLI/6/1/1,348, U.S. Naval Institute, www.usni.org, June 2015.

11 See Paul Rincon, 'UK Submarine Data De-Classified to Aid Climate Science', *BBC News*, www.bbc.co.uk, 23 February 2012.

12 For operational data on SCICEX, see the U.S. National Snow and Ice Data
    Center, https://nsidc.org.
13 For luxury submarines and submersibles see the 'Lifestyle' section of *Boat*
    International, www.boatinternational.com, accessed 28 May 2021.
14 For an analysis of FARC involvement in the drug trade see John Otis, 'The
    FARC and Colombia's Illegal Drug Trade', Wilson Center's Latin American
    Program, www.wilsoncenter.org, November 2014.

5 THE SUBMARINE AS FANTASY

1   H. P. Lovecraft, 'The Temple' [1925], in *The Complete Fiction of*
    H. P. Lovecraft (New York, 2014), p. 110.
2   Ibid., p. 121.
3   Adam Roberts, *Twenty Trillion Leagues Under the Sea* (London, 2014).
4   Alan Moore and Kevin O'Neill, illus., *The League of Extraordinary*
    Gentlemen (La Jolla, CA, 2000), vol. I.
5   Alan Moore and Kevin O'Neill, illus., *The League Of Extraordinary*
    Gentlemen (La Jolla, CA, 2003), vol. II.
6   Alan Moore and Kevin O'Neill, illus., *The League of Extraordinary*
    Gentlemen: The Black Dossier (La Jolla, CA, 2008).
7   See Joe Amato's comments in Joan Houlihan, 'Avant, Post-Avant,
    and Beyond', *Boston Comment*, www.bostoncomment.com, accessed
    28 May 2021.
8   Moore, *The League of Extraordinary Gentlemen*, vol. II.
9   Alan Moore and Kevin O'Neill, illus., *The League of Extraordinary*
    Gentlemen: The Tempest, no. 1 (La Jolla, CA, 2019)
10 K. W. Jeter, *Morlock Night* (Oxford, 1979).
11 Greg Moore, trans., *Arpeggio in Blue Steel* (Los Angeles, CA, 2010), vol. I.

6 THE SUBMARINE AND SEX

1   Morris J. MacGregor Jr, *Integration of the Armed Forces, 1940–1965*
    (Washington, DC, 2001), p. 87.
2   The CNO's 1995 report is cited in Krysten J. Ellis and Garold I. Munson,
    'Gender Integration on U.S. Navy Submarines: Views of the First Wave',
    MBA Professional Report, Naval Post-Graduate School, CA,
    https://calhoun.nps.edu, 2015, p. 14.
3   Patrick Robinson, *Kilo Class* (New York, 1998), pp. 377–8.
4   Michael Crichton, *Sphere* (New York, 1987), p. 79.
5   See Sophie Walton's ebook *Steampunk Submarine Sex Bundle* (2012),
    which includes 'Steampunk Submarine 1: Underwater Love'; 'Steampunk
    Submarine 2: Lesbian Ménage'; and 'Steampunk Submarine 3: SCUBA Sex'.
6   Patrick Robinson, *Seawolf* (New York, 2000), pp. 44–5.

7 Robinson, *Kilo Class*, pp. 82, 84–5.

8 Michael DiMercurio, *Emergency Deep* (New York, 2004), p. 436.

9 For detail on the Crittenden Report and subsequent U.S. Defense Department studies on gay soldiers in the military, which also found no practical or national security objections to their employment, see Shauna Miller, '50 Years of Pentagon Studies Support Gay Soldiers', *The Atlantic*, www.theatlantic.com, 20 October 2009.

10 For this and other details of life on a modern SSN see James Clark, 'Life on a Submarine: Raunchy, Cramped, and Occasionally Smells Like Sh*t', *Task and Purpose*, https://taskandpurpose.com, 7 October 2016.

11 Tyler Rogoway, 'Confessions of a U.S. Navy Submarine Officer', *Jalopnik*, https://jalopnik.com, 2 July 2015.

12 See report 'Submarine Hazing Centered on Homosexuality', *Fox News*, www.foxnews.com, 23 June 2012.

13 Within his social circle Mountbatten was widely accepted as bisexual, and both he and his wife, Edwina, conducted multiple extramarital affairs. The story about the Red House comes from his military driver at the time, and appears to be corroborated by FBI reports. See Grant Tucker, 'Lord Mountbatten's "Lust for Young Men" Revealed', *Sunday Times*, 18 August 2019.

14 Harvey Breit, 'In and Out of Books', *New York Times*, 3 April 1955.

CONCLUSION: THE END OF THE SUBMARINE?

1 Kyle Mizokami, 'The Sub of the Future Is a Drone Mothership Inspired by a Sperm Whale', *Popular Mechanics*, www.popularmechanics.com, 3 November 2018.

2 Stephen Chen, 'Will China's New Laser Satellite Become the "Death Star" for Submarines?', *South China Morning Post*, 1 October 2018.

3 Zachery Keck, 'China Has a New Plan to Hunt and Kill Navy Submarines', *National Interest*, https://nationalinterest.org, 27 September 2018.

4 Joe Pappalardo, 'How to Fight Submarines in the 21st Century', *Popular Mechanics*, www.popularmechanics.com, 28 January 2015.

5 For Operation Martillo, an international counter-smuggling effort led by U.S. Southern Command's Joint Interagency Task Force South, particularly its efforts to interdict narco-submarines, see Brian Anderson, 'The Hunt for Narco Subs', *Vice*, www.vice.com, 17 August 2015.

6 For CND's report on defence diversification while protecting jobs, see 'Trident and Jobs', *Campaign for Nuclear Disarmament*, https://cnduk.org, accessed 28 May 2021.

7 David Maab, 'William Morris Goes Atomic: A Provisional Memorial to Nuclear Disarmament', Research Online, Goldsmith University of London, http://research.gold.ac.uk, 3 December 2016.

8 See Nuclear Culture, https://nuclear.artscatalyst.org, accessed October 2019.

9 For the conclusion of Thompson, see 'Notes on Exterminism, The Last Stage of Civilization (Part 2)', www.versobooks.com, 28 December 2016.

10 Roger Morris, 'The Church Should Not Give Thanks that British Nuclear Weapons Are Still at Sea', *New Statesman*, www.newstatesman.com, 3 May 2019.

SELECT BIBLIOGRAPHY

Ballantyne, Iain, *The Deadly Trade: The Complete History of Submarine Warfare from Archimedes to the Present* (London, 2018)

Buchheim, Lothar-Günther, and J. Maxwell Brownjohn, trans., *U-Boat* (London, 1976)

Clancy, Tom, *The Hunt for Red October* (New York, 1985)

——, *Submarine: A Guided Tour Inside a Nuclear Warship* (New York, 1993)

Deighton, Len, *Blood, Tears and Folly: An Objective Look at World War II* (London, 1993)

Fullerton, Alexander, *Surface!* (London, 1953)

——, *Patrol to the Golden Horn* [1978] (New York, 2001)

Harris, Brayton, and Walter J. Boyne, ed., *The Navy Times Book of Submarines: A Political, Social, and Military History* (New York, 1997)

Hennessy, Peter, and James Jinks, *The Silent Deep: The Royal Navy Submarine Service since 1945* (London, 2015)

Hutchinson, Robert, *Jane's Submarines: War Beneath the Waves from 1776 to the Present Day* (New York, 2001)

MacGregor, Morris J. Jr, *Integration of the Armed Forces, 1940–1965* (Washington, DC, 2001)

Prebble, Stuart, *Secrets of the Conqueror: The Untold Story of Britain's Most Famous Submarine* (London, 2012)

Reeman, Douglas, *With Blood and Iron* (New York, 1965)

Roberts, Andrew, *The Storm of War: A New History of the Second World War* (London, 2010)

Verne, Jules, *Twenty Thousand Leagues Under the Sea* [1870] (London, 2014)

Weybrew, Benjamin B., *Report Number 917: History of Military Psychology at the U.S. Naval Submarine Medical Research Laboratory* (Groton, CT, 1979)

ACKNOWLEDGEMENTS

This one was my idea entirely and I did all of the work. There were a few people, though, who gave me encouragement and listened with apparent interest while I explained why such an unusual idea for a book might have value. So thanks to my daughters Ellie and Lizzie for reading some chapters and offering comments, and to various friends for letting me run on at length while explaining the basic idea. Your reactions, from polite bemusement to unexpected interest, helped clarify what I should and should not do.

In particular I must thank Simon Hannah, Elliot Murphy, Louis Bayman and John Merrick for feedback on an early draft, which led to real improvements in the final product.

PHOTO ACKNOWLEDGEMENTS

The author and publishers wish to express their thanks to the below sources of illustrative material and/or permission to reproduce it. Some locations of artworks are also given below, in the interest of brevity:

The American Civil War Museum, Richmond, VA: p. 21; from A. Frederick Collins and Virgil D. Collins, *The Boys' Book of Submarines* (New York, 1917), photo University of California Libraries: p. 62; Juan Corona/Shutterstock.com: p. 184; Granger/Shutterstock: pp. 138–9; ITV/Shutterstock: pp. 152–3; Library of Congress, Prints and Photographs Division, Washington, DC: pp. 18, 28–9, 65; Mic Smith Photography LLC/Alamy Stock Photo: p. 22; from H. A. Naber, *De ster van 1572: Cornelis Jacobsz. Drebbel* (Amsterdam, 1907): p. 8; National Archives at College Park, MD: pp. 25 (*bottom*), 57, 98 (photo JO2 Oscar Sosa), 168; Naval Education and Training Command, Pensacola, FL: p. 105; Naval History and Heritage Command, Washington, DC: pp. 24, 42–3, 43, 44, 45, 68, 131; The New York Public Library: p. 33; Eric Piermont/AFP via Getty Images: p. 188; Luis Robayo/AFP via Getty Images: p.145; Universal History Archive/Shutterstock: p. 124; University of South Florida, Tampa, FL: p. 123; U.S. Army/Arlington National Cemetery: p. 103 (photo Elizabeth Fraser); U.S. Navy: pp. 80–81 (photo John Narewski), 106–7 (photo SCPO Vien Nguyen), 132–3 (photo JOC Peter D. Sundberg), 143 (photo PO1 Michael B. Zingaro), 170 (photo PO2 Kelsey J. Hockenberger), 198–9 (photo PO1 Devin M. Langer); from Jules Verne, *Vingt mille lieues sous les mers* (Paris, 1871), photos Bibliothèque nationale de France, Paris: pp. 118, 119.

puuikibeach, the copyright holder of the image on p. 122, and William Warby, the copyright holder of the image on p. 136, have published them online under conditions imposed by a Creative Commons Attribution 2.0 Generic License. Readers are free to: share – copy and redistribute the material in any medium or format; adapt – remix, transform, and build upon the material for any purpose, even commercially. Under the following terms: attribution – you must give appropriate credit, provide a link to the license, and indicate if changes were made. You may do so in any reasonable manner, but not in any way that suggests the licensor endorses you or your use; no additional restrictions – you may not apply legal terms or technological measures that legally restrict others from doing anything the license permits.

INDEX

Page numbers in *italics* refer to illustrations